TURNING THE CAMERA INWARD:

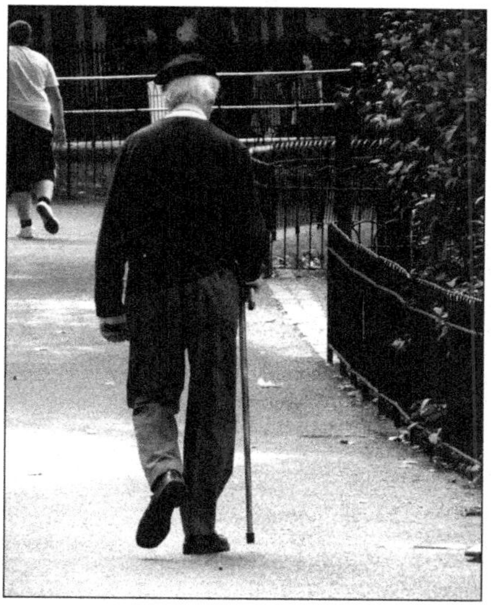

A search for
a photography of the self

DALE GARELL

Design by BookCreate
Seattle, Washington USA

Printed in USA

–

ISBN 978-0-9826637-2-1

FOREWORD

The photographer does not need to choose between competing alternatives. The "other" world document (i.e., the picture) and a self-revealing perspective of the person taking the photograph are both inevitable results of picture taking. Anyone willing to look inward as they take pictures of the outer world also has the opportunity to explore and achieve more insight into their own behavior and life story.

The "self" that photography captures might be defined, then, not only as an image of the person taking the picture rightly called a "selfie," but also as an interaction captured through the magic of picture taking itself, which is always a dialogue: between the photographer and his inner and outer worlds. Thus, taking a photograph permits an objective look at how these intimate relationships look when they are actually occurring.

When the camera is used to show not only what but how it sees, it is then the camera taking pictures from the standpoint of the self, and is always in relation to another. It is a continually unfolding process. The learning that occurs is to show not only others but oneself: how one sees and creates a clearer picture not only of the photographed subject, but of the photographer's way of being in the subject's world. If this is what it means to become a photographer of the self, how does one open up that perspective for everyday picture taking?

Turning the Camera Inward is an attempt to do just that.

> ~ John Beebe
> Author, *Integrity and Depth*;
> Past President, C.G. Jung Institute of San Francisco

CONTENTS

PREFACE

This is a book for those who love photography, enjoy taking photos, and are intrigued by the possibility that by doing so, they might learn more about themselves and find new ways to express their art. It means using imagination to tap into a part of their inner world. We can become artists of both our personal and work lives.

This book is my story and how my photography has evolved: about why photography has become important to my own process; about getting older; and about learning to accept realities and limitations as a person and a photographer. The book is also a reaffirmation, a summary of my work to date, a way of taking stock; and finally, it's a way to share why I am so hopeful about where my art is going and what I have to do to continue to learn.

One doesn't have to begin a new career as a photographer to use photography as a tool for self-learning. Self-learning is about starting a new creative process, testing the possibilities of learning, and discovering outcomes very different from expectations. It is about keeping going, being persistent and focused, and for me, it has been acting "as if" I was a photographer when I wasn't really sure I might ever become one.

The process itself of writing this book has altered its original plan for content. I have examined literally thousands of my pictures taken since I started in 2004. My review led me to look at the photos very differently and to select the ones

that illustrate the importance of turning the camera inward. I
continue to learn about myself.

I hope people will not only look at individual photos in this book,
but also at the body of my work as a whole. I'd like you to
think of the content of this book as several rooms of an exhibit
covering the last twelve years. I believe there is an internal
consistency: taking pictures of people in the streets; finding
scenes that can have universal meaning, looking for special
moments that evoke a sense of humor or whimsy or sadness or
curiosity; seeking and discovering images that touch me; and
finding pictures later on that highlight personal experiences in
my own life that add richness and texture.

> ~ Dale Garell
> Summer 2017

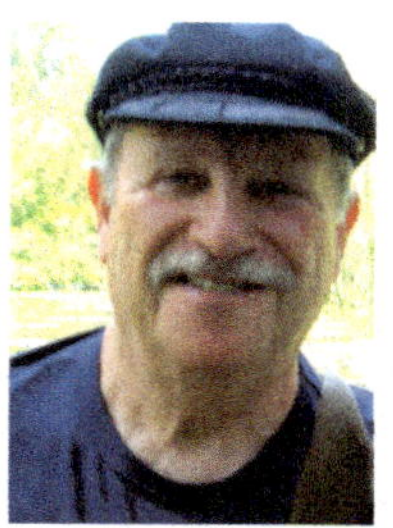

INTRODUCTION

Everyone takes pictures—that's for sure. We see waterfalls and mountaintops and grab our cell phones. We capture family reunions, holiday celebrations, and our kid's sporting events, seeing things we want to remember and we snap away. We buy new cameras to take on vacations, take shots of anything that moves, photograph sunsets and sunrises, monuments and buildings, and create gigabytes of photographic storage that clog our computers. It is hard to throw them out.

We view these photos afterward and learn how to enhance them—making them lighter or darker, and fine tuning, cropping, or blurring them intentionally—using today's computer-assisted techniques that make it possible to turn out high-quality work that pleases us.

Some of us attend classes to understand the complexities of picture taking: We learn how to use f-stops, manual exposures, and time-lapse settings, and how to make digital 4K movies at the touch of a button. We go on photo junkets, watch educational how-to tapes, and send instantaneous pictures over the Internet to family, friends, and others who enjoy them or say they do. We take pictures of ourselves at a moment's notice, personally memorializing our presence at a special event or with a celebrity who agrees to become our subject.

We Instagram (the verb), upload to Facebook, touch-up for Match.com. We are probably the most visually represented people in history. On occasion, we take a special photo, and cherish and remember the details of how it happened. We take multiple pictures at a time, sift through them to pick the best, create books, wall hangings, cards, and calendars. We are a camera-carrying culture (and phones with cameras, too) out to

take pictures of everything and anything for a very good reason
. . . we can.

Truly, anyone can become a photographer and sometimes an
excellent one.

———————————

It wasn't always so.

Joseph Nicéphore Niépce took the first known photograph in
1826 in the Burgundy region of France, *View from the Window
at Le Gras*.(1) The first commercial camera was developed in
1839 by Louis Daguerre, making permanent pictures with a
technique that became known as the daguerreotype, adding
mercury vapor to polished silver-plated copper.(2) In 1867
Carleton Watkins took pictures of new dams being built along
the Columbia River, reportedly hauling more than two thousand
pounds of photographic equipment on horseback to get to
the right spot at the right time.(3) He surely never imagined a
camera that could fit into his pocket, take multiple exposures to
be sent immediately via the Internet anywhere in the world, and
not fade over time.

Photography was originally shunned as art by both museums
and collectors alike. Curiosities of the nineteenth and early
twentieth century, it was an expensive hobby for the very rich,
made popular by lifelike portraiture, newsworthy additions to
narrative reporting and became an asset to marketing and
fashion. It was not long before artists who paint began using
photography as their starting point, though their work was not
thought to be original and they were labeled copyists.

Van Deren Coke's classic book about the important

relationships between artists and photography, *The Painter and the Photograph*, published in 1934, pointed out that "today's art historians . . . generously fail to recognize that photography has, ever since 1839, been to a host of artists both a source and an influence." Commenting on photography and art, he added: "Throughout the history of art it has been art itself—in all its forms—that have inspired art." (4)

David Hockney, who co-authored a recent book with Martin Gayford, *A History of Pictures*, makes the strong argument that "whether they are made by brush, camera or digital program, and no matter whether they are on cave walls or computer screens, first and foremost they are all pictures." (5)

50 Photographers You Should Know, published in 2011, provides brief biographies of famous photographers, tracing the overall history of picture taking and reiterates the common perception at the time: photography was not fully recognized as art, but as a craft. (6) Jeffrey's *How to Read a Photograph: Lessons Learned from Master Photographers* also provides biographies and analysis of over 160 years of their work. (7) Of interest is that the first photography exhibit at the Louvre (that of Cartier-Bresson's work) wasn't held until 1966.

Today, photographs are highly prized throughout the art world, selling at increasingly astronomical sums. "Phantom," a recent landscape photo by Peter Lik, sold for $6.5 million in 2014, according to *Artnet News*. (8) Photographs are finally accepted as fine art—recognized for the skills of the photographer and the qualities of the printing process; by the composition, colors, and designs; the ink and paper used; and the creative and unique possibilities of the photographic field in and of itself.

The introduction of the compact Leica 35 mm camera in 1925 started the modern photojournalism era by making it possible to immediately capture views from many perspectives and take multiple sequential pictures of related events as a continuing story. With the advent of the cell phone, "citizen" journalists now take quality photos at the scene of any breaking news event, often supplanting newspaper photographers as first responders.

The field of photojournalism, in its narrowest sense, uses images to tell a news story, and has been described as "the art or practice of communicating news by photographs, especially in magazines. It has come to include documentary photography, social documentary photography, street photography, and celebrity photography." (9) Street photography, its definitions and relationships, are detailed in a scholarly work by Scott. (10)

Still famous today, and perhaps the best known exhibit of black-and-white photos ever, is *The Family of Man*, curated by Edward Steichen and held at the New York Museum of Modern Art in 1955. This collection of 503 photos from 68 countries toured the world and was subsequently published in a classic book. (11)

Henri Cartier-Bresson (1908–2004), one of the greatest photographers of his day and arguably the father of modern photojournalism, defined photography for himself in *The Decisive Moment*, 1952, (12), New York, Simon & Schuster, introduction, xiv):

"Photography is the simultaneous recognition, in a fraction of a second, of the significance of an event as well as of a precise organization of forms which give that event its proper expression."

By the twenty-first century, technology had automated virtually every part of the visual process—from focus to final product, from digital to 3-D to virtual reality, the mechanics of taking

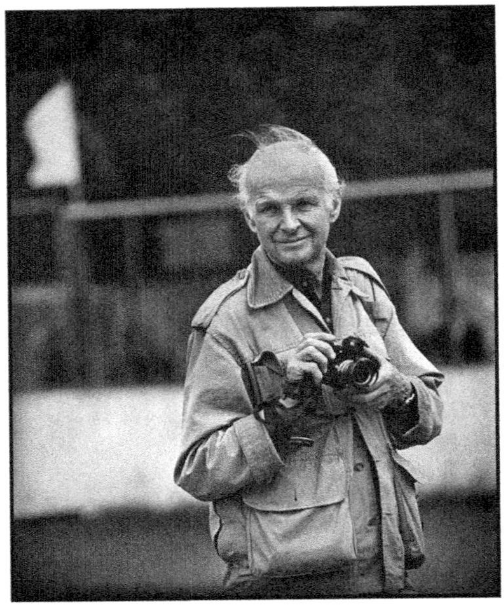

Henri Cartier-Bresson,
Moscow 1947

Courtesy of Magnum Photos

pictures have undergone continuous transformations with expected improvements every year in miniaturization, expanded storage, resolution, and transmission of work to computers and printers at a distance.

What hasn't changed are the people who use them.

———

I have asked myself, why write this book? Why add another coffee-table book, outdated immediately, like so many photography books today that soon go to the back of the bookcase and gather dust, waiting for their place at a future garage sale? Certainly, there are many skilled photographers around, writers and historians chronicling the art of photography. There are books about finding the right settings to achieve the right lighting effect; books about best ways to compose a picture, the science of photography, and complexities of camera physics and its properties; how- to books that describe post-production techniques; and others that write about creating portfolios, marketing, selling, and exhibiting photography. (10–20) It is certainly not necessary to rehash and reframe.

Most photography books are picture books, limited to pictures with very little text, or they are a biography of the photographer with supporting text needed to emphasize or understand a particular technique or the circumstances involved at the time, frequently letting the pictures speak for themselves. Few photographers describe the impact of taking pictures and what it's like to become a photographer.

Rarely do photographers describe changes occurring in themselves, the personal impact of becoming observers of others while trying to capture the human condition, nor do photographers write about the emotional impact of taking pictures as individuals. Each photographer's own story is unique, determined by the visual choices of where they pointed their cameras. By understanding more about the photographer, we add to our own understanding as viewers, and more importantly, why the photographer may have selected a particular event or presentation.

Édouard Boubat's book of photography, *It's a Wonderful Life*, provides in depth personal disclosures of whom he might be. We learn about Boubat, the person, through thoughtful quotes selected throughout the book to match his photos and from his introductory remarks, "Lights in the Darkroom:"

"When I take a photo, I feel like a young man again, ageless . . . At the sublime moment of taking a photograph, there is nothing else to wait for: it is there. Time has melted in an instant. Some have invented eternity; I am simply a modern inventor.

When the photographer "connects" with his subject, photography becomes art, a link between the photographer's eye and the universal value and meaning of his art. An awareness of the self may accentuate and improve the meaning of the photo being taken. In the process this increases the special moments that help all of us understand and learn more about ourselves and the world we live in.

Consider the impact of capturing a previously unrealized or spontaneous moment that truly touches us all. The 2016 photo of a young Iraqi boy sitting in the back of an emergency vehicle became a symbol of the pain and suffering of a whole generation caught in the crossfire of a civil war without end. What was going through the mind of the photographer who took that photo? Wouldn't you like to know?

Henri Cartier-Bresson said this about the special relationship he believed existed between himself and the potential universality of his photography:

"I believe that, through the act of living, the discovery of oneself is made concurrently with the discovery of the world around us which can mold us, but which can also be affected by us. A balance must be established between these two worlds—the one inside and the one outside us. As a result of a constant reciprocal process, both these worlds come to form a single one. And it is this world that we must communicate."

"In whatever one does, there must be a relationship between the eye and the heart. One must come to one's subject in a

pure spirit. One must be strict with oneself. There must be time for contemplation, for reflection about the world and the people about one. If one photographs people, it is their inner look that must be revealed."

(From an interview of Cartier-Bresson by Dorothy Newman, as quoted in his obituary of August 3, 2004, *NY Times,* Michael Kimmelman. (19)

In 2000, I retired and moved from Los Angeles to the Oregon Coast after an academic pediatric medical career of nearly forty years. I had known Iris Litt professionally as a pediatrician from the time of the earliest days of the emerging field of Adolescent Medicine. Iris and I would see each other at meetings as colleagues among the founders of the field. She had lost her husband in 2000. My wife, Aggie, had died suddenly in the spring of 2003. In 2004 we unexpectedly fell in love and were married that summer. We settled in San Francisco as she was still working at Stanford University. A year later, on our first trip to Paris together in 2005, something occurred that was also totally unexpected. I fell in love again, this time with Paris!

What I loved most about Paris were the people, going about their everyday lives, baguettes under arms, children in uniforms leaving school, sweethearts embracing, people with disabilities crossing the street, downtrodden characters with outstretched hands, vendors selling food and souvenirs, street cleaners in green with brooms pushing water and waste down the streets, bicycles and dogs everywhere, smokers, tourists dragging luggage in search of hotels. I was surprised and touched by what I saw that went beyond the usual tourist photo-ops I had been taking.

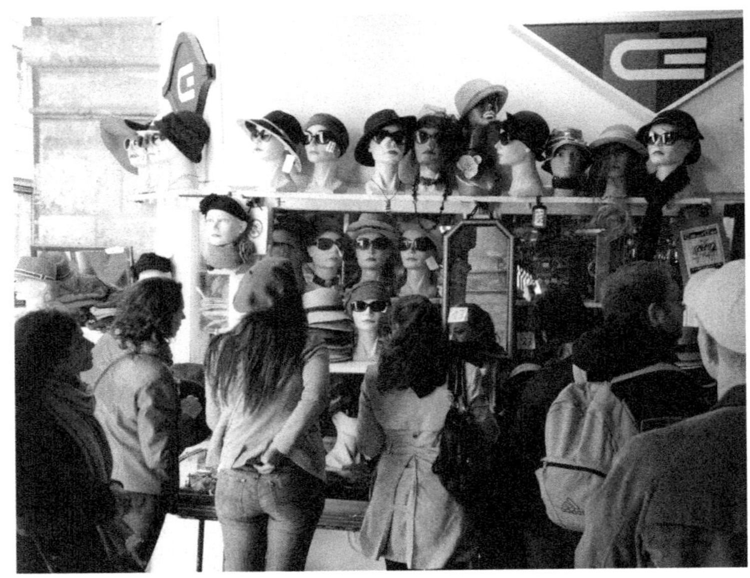

Le Marais, Paris

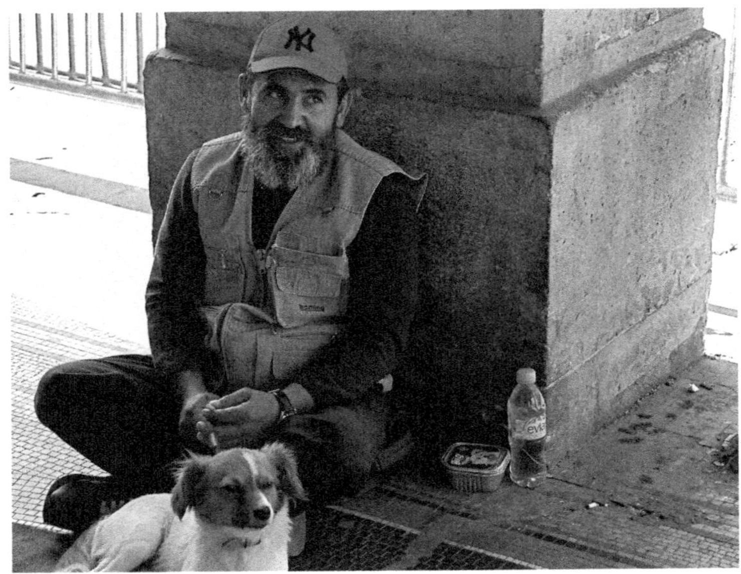

Rue Rivoli, Paris

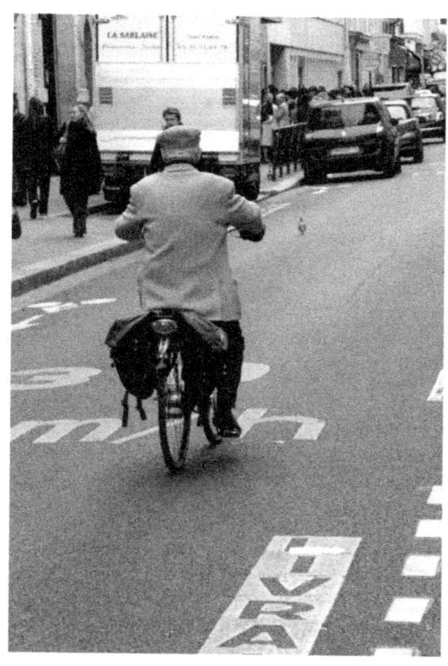

Rue Cler, Paris

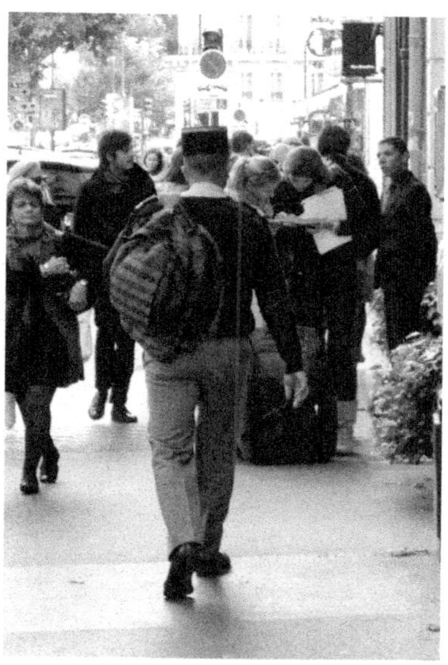

Boulevard Saint-Germain, Paris

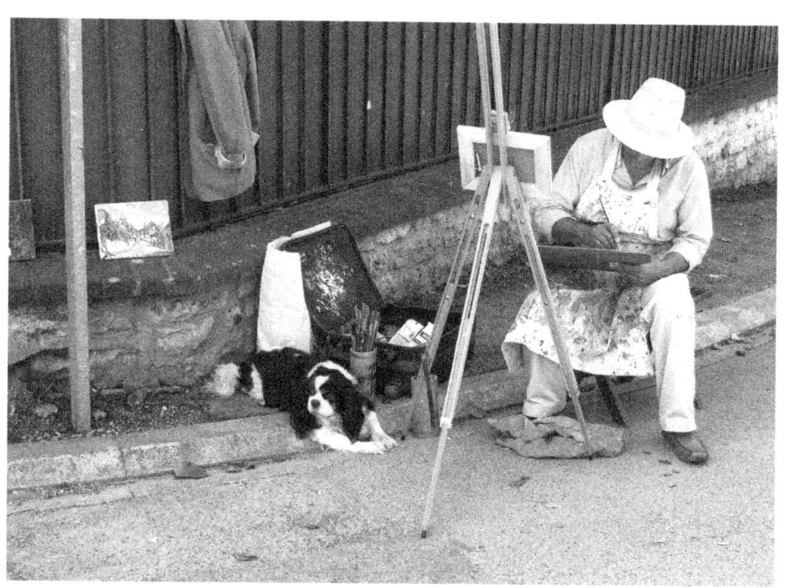

Giverny, France

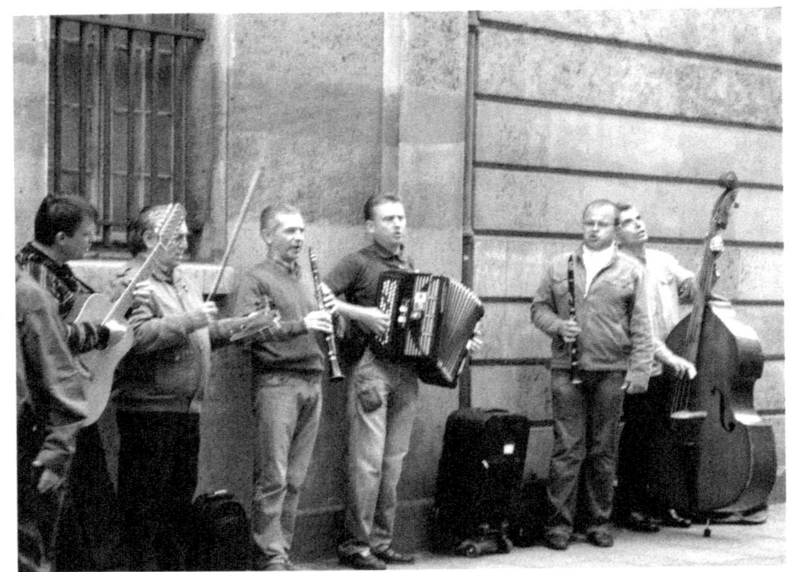

Le Marais, Paris

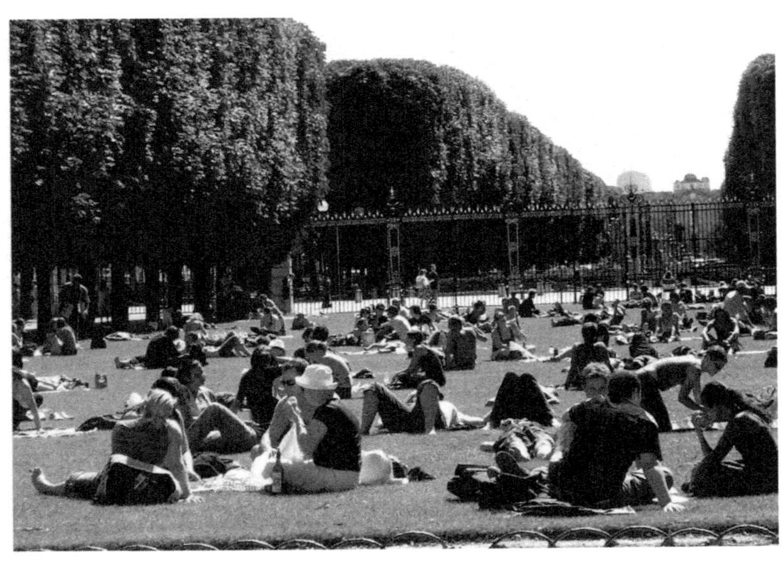

Luxembourg Gardens, Paris

Photography became my second career during the first few years of our marriage, and an integral part of what were to become annual trips to Paris. I learned about the challenges of taking black-and-white pictures; finding the courage and submitting photos for juried shows; the hard work of preparing and carrying out an exhibit; searching and finding a professional photography lab to fine tune and finish photos; hiring an agent; creating a website (wwwdalegarellphotography.com); self-publishing; and starting to think of myself as a photographer.

My original goal was to encourage viewers to look more deeply inside themselves while viewing photos in my collections—to find those that uniquely touched them and enabled them to experience special moments, i.e., "moving pictures" that have the ability to become a kind of photographic "Rorschach."

To my thinking, it is the responsibility of the photographer to stimulate meaningful dialogue. A photo should ask of its first-time viewer: What does this photograph do for you? Does it bring up memories in your own life? Does it have meaning to you? Why does it touch you? What do you like about it?

Similar questions might also arise in the photographer upon further reflection: Why did I take this picture? What does it do for me? What memories does it evoke in my life? What meaning arises from the photo? Why does it touch me? Why do I like it?

The objectivity of the photographer to report what he sees should be balanced by encouraging a photographer's self-reflection, learning to observe himself taking the picture, and discovering what emotional changes arise spontaneously— quite the opposite from impartially reporting visual events without emotion, so totally objective when reporting life from a distance and often lacking any possible human connections between the artist and the subject.

The photographer need not be faced with these two competing alternatives. It is possible to do BOTH!

Anyone willing to look inward when taking pictures also has the opportunity to explore and achieve more insight into his own behavior and an awareness of his own life story. "A photography of the self" might be defined as *the interactions between a photographer and his inner and outer worlds, permitting a fuller understanding of the learning that occurs when the camera is turned inward, by providing insight and awareness and therefore creating a clearer vision, thus enhancing the skills and beauty of a photographer's life and art.*

What does it mean to aspire to become a photographer of the self?

I see better now than before I started taking photos: the little things that are suddenly of interest to me, that somehow show themselves as I look more closely at the world around me, that make me laugh or cry or make me pause for a moment to think more fully. I become more alive when I am taking pictures. I am in awe of the people who are in my photos and of what they can teach me about myself, why it is important on an internal level to have a camera in hand to photograph the world spontaneously. I hold the strong belief there is much to learn about human nature through the process of taking pictures and by understanding personal challenges by looking at our own lives through the lens of a camera.

Photography, as an added tool, makes it possible to observe how others live their lives, find possible universal applications, and seek truths for our own personal life stories. Thus, a photography of the self adds special meaning to the photographer as well.

At the age of eighty-one, I realize that I do not want to be a photojournalist at the scene of a major disaster, a war, or a historical event. I know I won't win a Pulitzer Prize or have a picture on page one of the *New York Times*. My picture taking makes me a better observer, lets me have fun, and allows me to weave my love of photography into the changes and challenges of the later part of my life.

I am convinced that photography need not involve the battlefield or street scenes of individuals, but evolves from capturing the beauty of the moment—rain as it falls, cascading down a river; a flower in bloom; wheat in movement; a chair or a bowl of fruit, a street scene of two people standing at a curb waiting to cross a busy Paris street arm in arm, or an abstract photo enhanced to provide new visual dimensions. Photography then, is an art of the moment, when the artist, using a camera, captures something that speaks to him or her, and reaches inside to touch a special feeling, evoke a memory or discover an unknown thought rising to the surface. This gut reaction to our world helps us understand a little bit better, find meaning in what we do, and achieve a moment when time stands still. That is a photography of the self!

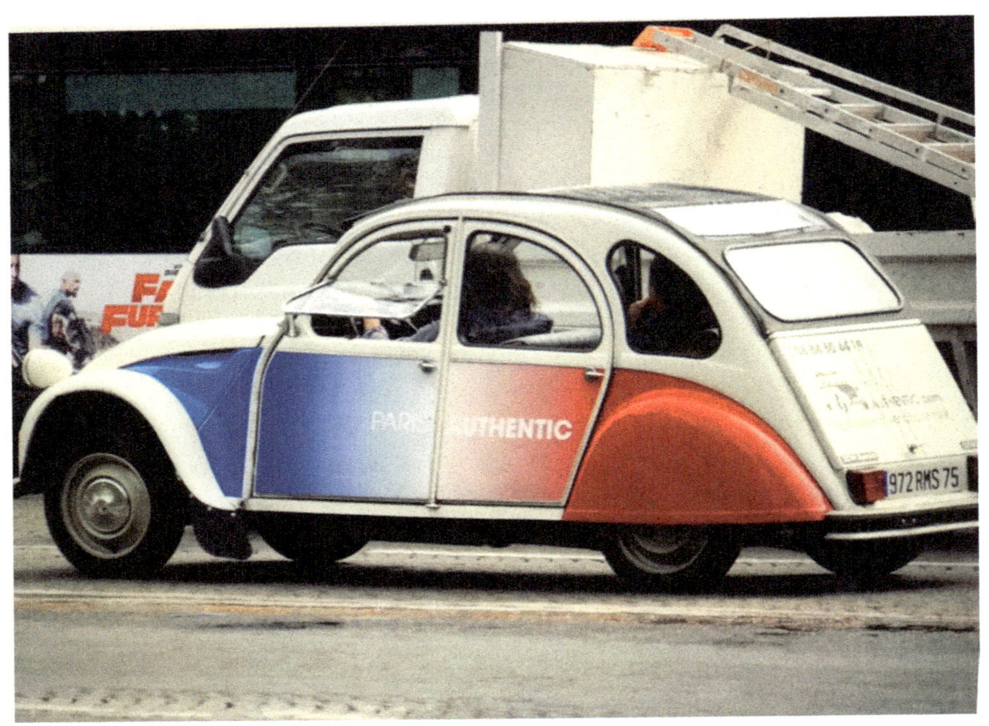

Deux Chevaux (Citreon), Paris

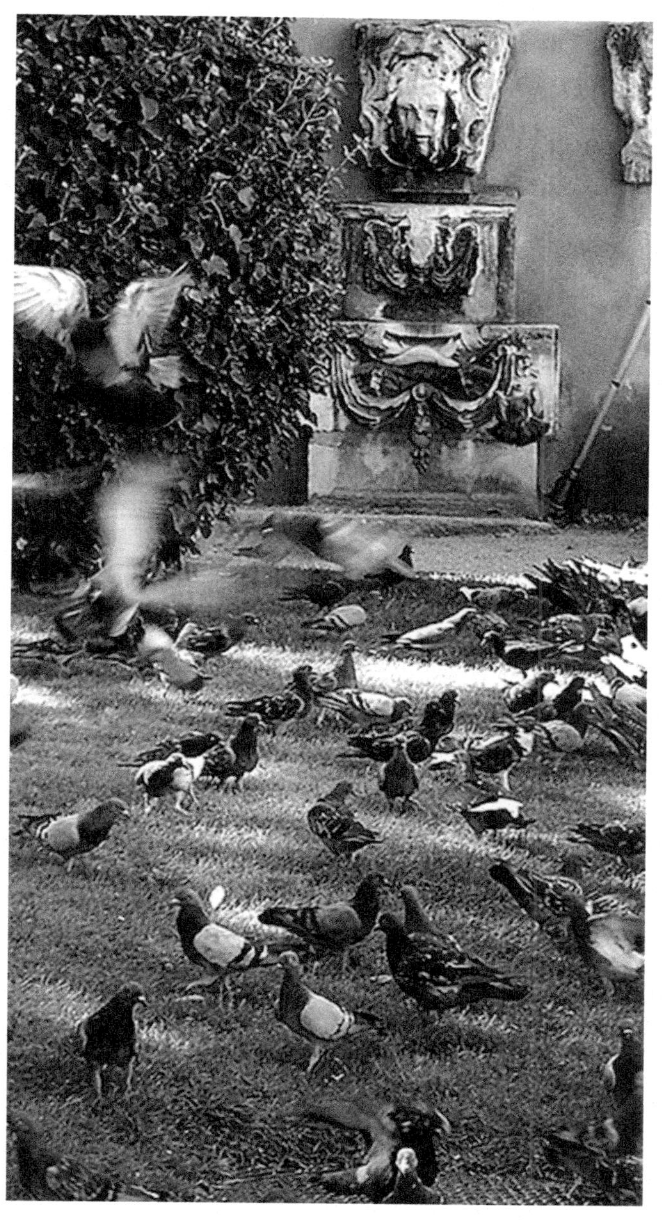

Le Marais, Paris

SECTION I

**Early Work,
Discovery
and Success
(2005–2011)**

CHAPTER ONE

Are You Sure Ansel Adams
Started This Way?

Taking pictures was an occasional activity for me earlier in my life without much thought about whether anyone beyond my family would ever see them. My cameras were simple—the point-and-shoot variety—and they were a way to document that I had been on a vacation or participated in a family event. My 4x6s were handed to me in drugstore envelopes, opened, placed in a drawer, and rarely looked at again. I probably should have thrown them out.

At first, my photos of Paris were very ordinary: famous park scenes and cobblestone streets, classic French cars, people in love, attractions like the Tour de France, outdoor monuments, museums, and galleries. I took a lot of pictures of tourists taking pictures of other tourists. Living in Paris several weeks a year changed my picture taking. I ran out of scenes. So, it seemed only natural to separate tourist shots from other pictures that would soon capture my interest.

When we returned to California after our first trip in 2005, my color photos were transferred to the computer screen, edited and cropped, and put into two categories: pictures of our

travels together and everything else. It was roughly 75/25. The
"75" were screened and sent to family waiting to see our trip
to France the year after our marriage. Many prints, intended
for unfilled albums, became digital tour guides and family files.
The other "25" remained untouched, ready to be filed away. For
what purpose, I wasn't really sure.

I had been reading about the history of photography and the
early twentieth-century photographers of France. Their work
preceded the advent of color, and were limited to black and
white or sepia tones. They were beautiful to me. I found myself
admiring composition and techniques, imagining what they might
have done if they were alive today. It was also fun to imagine
what pictures I might have taken had I lived during their time.

A few days later, I pulled out the "other 25" file again, looked
at the color photos, and on impulse, clicked on the button
making them into black and whites. How much I liked these
monochromatic pictures—they looked even better to me
without color! The shades of gray, the unexpected textures
and subtle highlights of composition focused more on daily
activities, spontaneous without posing. I was struck by the
blurred similarities between my newly changed black and
whites and the earlier photos of Paris. It seemed as if I really
had traveled back to that era, taken pictures, and returned to
the present.

As I read more about these early photographers, I became
inspired to follow in their footsteps and intentionally try to
capture life in today's France by walking the streets of Paris,
imagining stories, and trying to take pictures I hoped might help
me discover more about everyday people. My subjects wouldn't
be posed or looking straight into the camera. They wouldn't
be artificial or staged, but would be snapshots of spontaneous
acts of living. What were these people thinking? Feeling? What
were their lives like? If I was able to have a conversation with
them, what might they tell me? What were their stories?

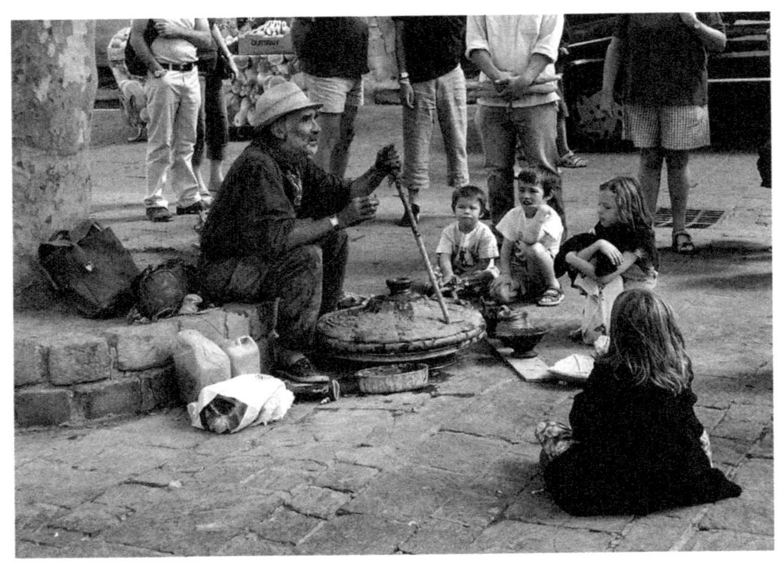

The Potter, Uzes, France

The next time we were in Paris, I was out again taking pictures without much thought, randomly working the crowds with camera in hand, taking lots of photos, missing a few "great" shots because I wasn't camera-ready; but I was keeping an open mind, letting my camera work randomly without attention to detail or scripted scenes. No instant editing: taking spontaneous street scenes and hoping for special moments similar to those that had preceded me eighty-five years earlier.

I decided I needed to find someone who might be able to give me honest feedback. Were they any good? Was there a message? Would people like them? I found an art manager-consultant in the Carmel area where we were living and made an appointment to see her.

Shirley (Polovy) looked at my work without comment, sifting through color pictures and a few of the black and whites, noncommittal. Thoughtfully, she asked, "What is your passion?"

This was followed by, "What work do you think you'd like to pursue further?" And then, "Choose!"

I told her more about the black and whites and she said, "Put together a portfolio of five to ten of your photos that show your best work." The next time we met, she looked over what I had brought. "I think I have somewhere for you to exhibit your photography."

The Davenport Exhibit (2010)

The place she had in mind was a popular restaurant and small hotel in Davenport, California, a seaside town north of Santa Cruz on Highway 1 that had exhibits of local artists and photographers on display in their restaurant.

It was raining the day we arrived with a car loaded with ten framed photos, not knowing where they would be placed or any details about the installation.

I found a hotel clerk at the front desk, who pointed me in the direction of the restaurant. Inside, there was no one to help, no one in charge. A staff person finally walked through the door, showed me a ladder, and said I could hang them there, gesturing toward the vacant walls of the restaurant. After a trip back to a hardware store in Santa Cruz in the pouring rain, I returned with the necessary hammer, picture hooks, and wire. I hung them myself, standing back to admire my black-and-white photos of the streets of Paris.

The manager arrived fifteen minutes later, saw the pictures hanging above tables, near the front door, and around serving areas. He looked at me, then looked back again at the photos, finally shaking his head. I asked him if there was something wrong. "I thought there would be pictures of the seashore, the sand, and beautiful trees of the coast of California," he said. "They're just pictures of Europe."

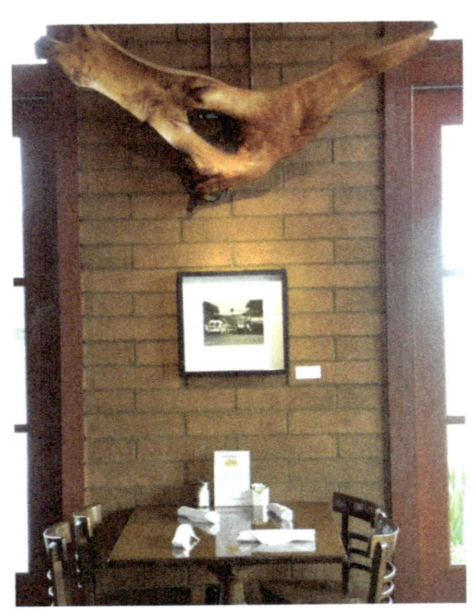

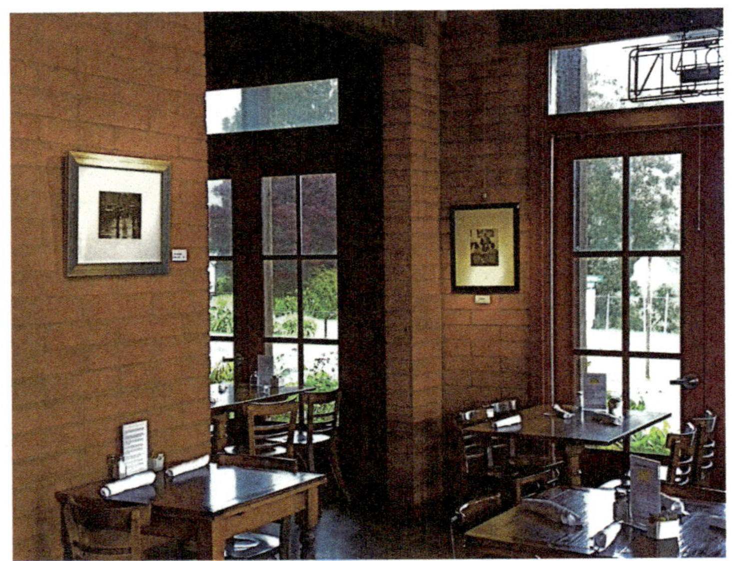

Davenport, California

He didn't make me take them down then, but a few weeks later Shirley called to say that the exhibit was over and I should pick them up. As I was pulling them off the walls, I started laughing: Do you suppose, I thought, this is really how Ansel Adams got his start?

My first exhibit turned out to be one of my best learning experiences:

1. The exhibit isn't ready until the pictures are hung; sometimes, you're the only one there to hang them.

2. Not everyone will like your work; be sure they are seen before they are hung.

3. Laughter is a great healer; don't take yourself too seriously.

4. I am not interested in taking pictures of the seashore.

CHAPTER TWO

First Exhibits in California

(2010–2011)

Having recovered from my inaugural showing, Shirley told me not to be discouraged; she had identified three other possible local exhibits in the Monterey area. My peer-reviewed submission to the Pacific Grove Art Center was accepted for an exhibit of twenty photos, to be hung fortunately by someone else in one of their galleries. The art director of the gallery at the Sunset Center in Carmel also approved a thirty-photo exhibit. Having seen my work, she wanted black-and-white photos taken solely from the backs of the subjects. The third, placed in the hallways of a local government office building in Seaside, California, was also approved and was a showing of four photos, along with the works of two other artists. Another curator-reviewed exhibit of thirty photos was held at Stanford in 2011 as well.

My immediate question became how to prepare for an exhibit.

Finding a Professional Printing Lab

Mastering Photoshop was no easy task. While many have learned the techniques of this wonderful software, it was not for me. This was complicated, not for amateurs I thought, and certainly not for someone like myself who didn't use the software every day. Nor was I ready to invest in a sophisticated photo printer at home, taking the time to learn how to use seven different kinds of ink and special archival paper. Not only did I need to make postproduction refinements to the photos and alter their sizing, but also needed to find someone who could do a little magic with my photographic effort, i.e., make improvements without changing the composition or intent of the art. I wanted to create a high quality product suitable for professional exhibits as the standard for my work.

A well-known commercial printing service in San Francisco, Urban Digital Color, specializes in photography and seemed to suit my needs. Their website, www.urbandigitalcolor.com, with its array of specialized printing equipment, technical know-how, and clientele was impressive. I wondered if they also did black-and-white photographic preparation and fine art photo printing. I called and confirmed an appointment to prepare for my first exhibit in Pacific Grove.

With flash drive in hand, I walked into the Urban Digital Color lab. Gigantic color photos were on the walls with abstract designs and flourishes. A young receptionist greeted me and began sizing me up. I told her of my appointment and she pointed me to a back room full of Macs and a group of large tables with work in progress on display.

That was where I met Troy. He was busy at his screen, not looking up from his work. When he finally saw me said, "Let's see what you've got," shoving my flash disk into the slot. It seemed like an hour or so as he moved through the photos I had selected for my exhibit.

"What do you want me to do?"

"Fix them," I said flatly.

"What do you want me to fix?"

I didn't have a ready answer. All I knew was, it just wasn't right. I really didn't know enough to answer him.

In retrospect, he was asking all the right questions about sizing and touch-up and shades of this and that. I told him proudly that I had been accepted for an exhibit in Monterey for my black-and-white photos and needed help with the final preparation of my work. He kept asking more questions I couldn't answer. Finally, he got up, pointed me to one of the large tables, went away and came back with ten different types of archival paper and asked me which one I liked. I picked two and then he went on to ask about the type of archival ink I wanted to use. "What is archival ink?" I asked. He didn't reply. He just copied my disk, and told me to come back when the proofs were ready.

I left knowing I hadn't really carefully thought about what I wanted for the exhibit. How did I want my work to be seen? What was I trying to do? When I returned a few weeks later, it was more of the same, now with work that I could see in front of me that looked like I knew what I was doing.

Troy wasn't going to answer any of the questions for me. I was the artist—the photographer—it was my work and I had to tell him what I wanted. He taught me to make decisions about shades of black and white, what paper I wanted, the right ink to choose, and how to achieve the effect I had hoped for. It was like taking the original photo all over again, now seen by someone who could technically make changes but needed to know what I liked and what I wanted. He wasn't going to let me back away. They were my photos, not his. He was relentless.

A few more weeks and I had the finished photos and a new flash disk in hand. I thanked Troy profusely and paid the receptionist who wished me luck with a knowing smile.

Off to Aaron Brothers for professional framing. I had chosen same-size narrow black frames, with off-white mats to match the photo paper. Each photo was given a name, a date when it was taken, signed, and numbered, and was ready for the show.

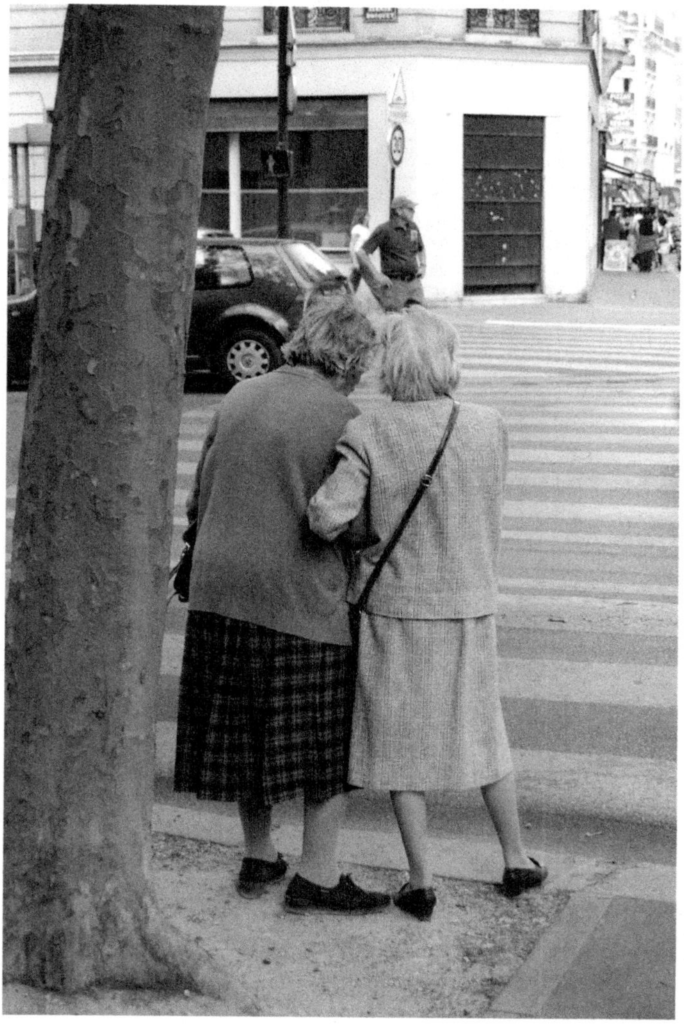

Friends; 7th Arrondissement, Paris

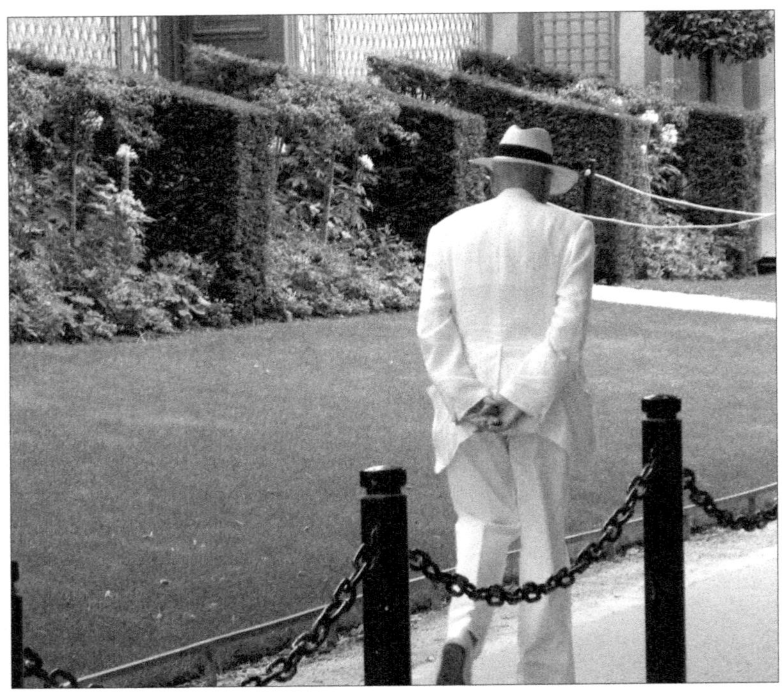

Man in a White Suit, Luxembourg Gardens, Paris

My Camera

I don't see in black and white when I take pictures. Nor do I use a digital camera made exclusively for black and white photography. These monochromatic cameras, i.e., digital cameras that take original pictures only in black and white, are expensive ($7,000 to more than $40,000) and are out of my price range. I have been told they assure the most successful monochromatic photos. But some digital cameras also have a monochromatic mode so that photos can be originally shot in black and white by changing the setting. Or, if you have a digital camera that shoots in JPEG or RAW (21), it is possible to use Photoshop, Lightroom, or other software and later convert original color photos to black and white. See Digital Photo Pro magazine, May 4, 2015 (22), an issue devoted to black-and-white photography and other reference material for more details about monochromatic digital cameras and related software.

Pacific Grove (2010)

When I arrived for the installation a few days before the opening, twenty photos carried in the back of my car, I was pleased to find that the gallery had an official picture hanger. He showed me the gallery and helped me place the photos on the floor ready to be hung on the four walls around us; they were then hung carefully and professionally. On one wall was the name of my show, People I've Seen, along with my name, an enlarged picture of an old man taken in St. James Park in London, and stacks of programs on a card table with wall-ready photos for the exhibit.

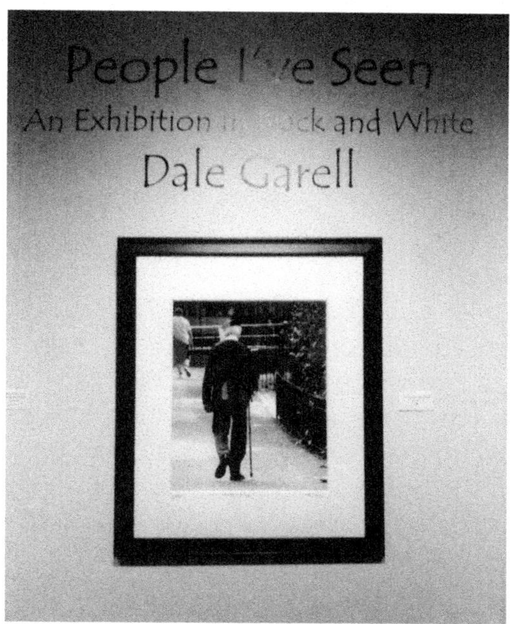

*Pacific Grove,
California*

Newly printed business cards in my pocket, we parked, I said a few last minute prayers, and we walked up the flight of stairs into the gallery for opening night. We were early, sampled the wine and cheese, and had a chance to walk around to see the exhibits of the other two artists who turned out to be painters, confirming that I was still competing with paintings and pictures of Monterey pines, bougainvillea, and the crashing waves of Big Sur.

The crowd arrived, roaming around the photos on the walls, stopping, looking around some more, moving on to the next photo. I stayed in the background, hoping for some response and wondering what they were thinking. A few actually stayed, while others ventured into the other galleries.

"I like it," said a man as I walked toward him, who had been looking at one picture for some time. "What do you like?" I asked, realizing that he didn't really know who I was. "It makes me think about my father," he said with a tear in his eye. Another woman remarked about another photo that it reminded her of a time when she was a little child. A third, "Where are the pictures of the Monterey Bay? The seals?" Finally, someone said, "Did you do these? They are wonderful!" More than seventy-five people attended the opening and while not always connecting, it was touching to see how many stopped and looked.

The Sunset Center (2011)

It was a similar experience at the Sunset Center, a community art and entertainment center in Carmel. The curator wanted a different orientation to my photos, asking that all thirty to be shown would be taken from the back. It took a little doing, but I was able to find them; and with the help of Troy and Aaron Brothers, had another month-long solo exhibit. "An interesting perspective," she said, "to imagine what people are thinking

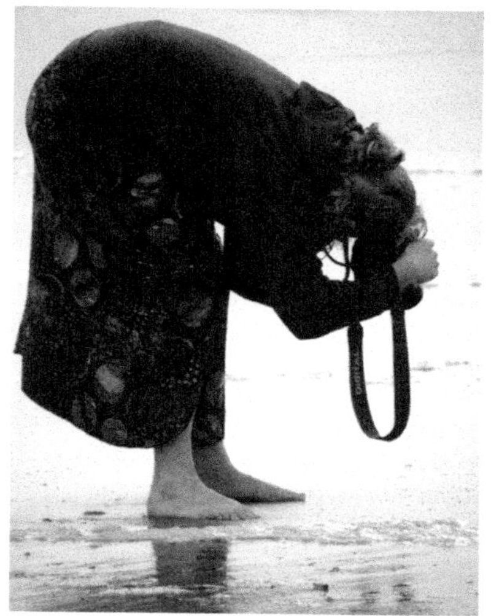 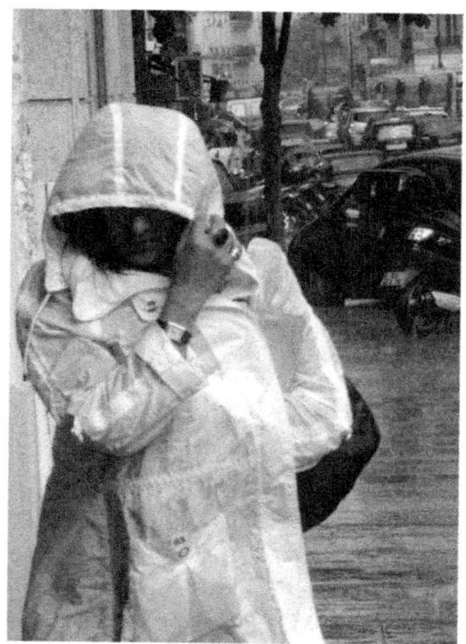

Manzanita, Oregon   *Champs-Élysées, Paris*

when they see only the backs of people without the visual clues of facial expression."

The opening again offered an opportunity to talk with people and watch their observations. This was a one-person reception so there was no competition, with more than thirty photos, hors d'oeuvres, and white wine, courtesy of myself. Including photos prepared for showing, framing, and food and wine for the opening reception, exhibits were getting expensive. But, it was another opportunity for people to comment and a reaffirmation that my work was acceptable. Cost didn't really matter. Visibility and experience, I told myself. After thirty days, none had sold.

Seaside California Government Center

More of the same, four black and whites, shared hallway space with other artists. The routine was getting very familiar: people love art in public spaces, and walls are available for showing if you know whom to call or where to inquire.

The question was whether there was enough payoff in return to merit the cost of preparing and handling the photographs. I knew that my work was being well received. Was that enough?

Besides learning how to hang my own photos, I also became a framer—my black-and-white photos, painfully placed in simple 16" x 20" black frames, was my specialty. I put up a website (www.dalegarellphotography.com), determined a price range for my work, held an open studio exhibit in our home, made business cards, incorporated as Dale Garell Photography LLC, started a self-publishing program over the next three

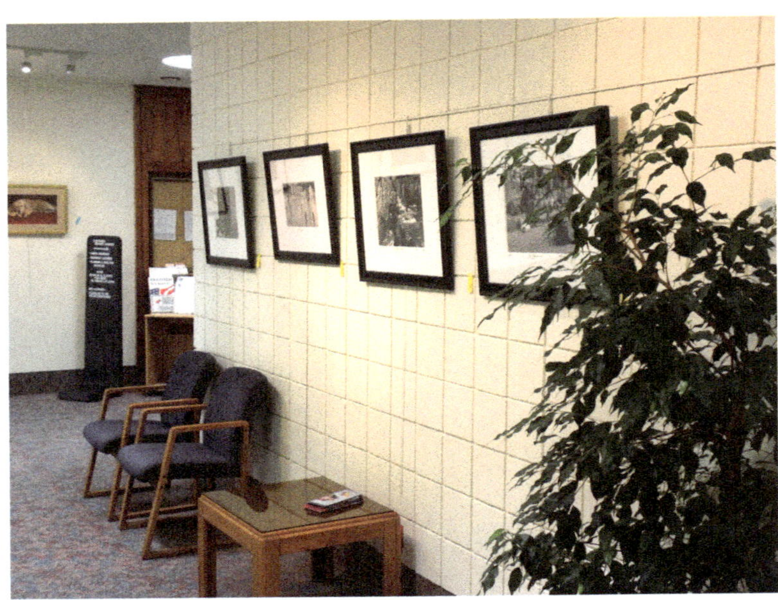

Seaside, California

years, and published four softbound photo books. I decided this was going to be a serious effort on my part. I surely didn't think I was really a photographer yet, only someone who took pictures. I was still searching for an audience who might like my work, trying to find my own style of expression, and hoping that maybe one day a national art gallery or a museum might want to exhibit my work. In the meantime, I decided I might as well act "as if" I was a photographer. It never occurred to me that photography might teach me about myself.

Lessons Learned

1. If at first you don't succeed . . .

2. Having a resource for finalizing and professionally preparing photographs is the difference between a show and an exhibit; quality photo enhancing, archival paper and ink, framing and hanging create the overall impression of an established body of work, showing the serious nature and commitment of the artist to his art. It is a very different experience than presenting a single photograph.

3. Thoughtful preparation, thematic orientation, preparation of work into a professional format, and seeking professional advice for an exhibit requires more than a one-person effort.

4. Professional help does not involve abdication of responsibility. These were my photos and I had to decide the purpose of my exhibit, which photos to include, what I wanted to convey, and how they were to be presented.

5. Professional photography is an expensive activity; the least expense is the camera. Costs for production and preparation of the photographs, framing, and professional display as well as opening reception costs are costly if you want to do it right. To be involved in serious photography is

expensive. All told, I spent more than $5,000 that first year; having a budget is important and recognizing personal limits for cost versus return is important.

6. Digital cameras take their photos in JPEG or RAW format, with varying amounts of information. RAW contains all of the information, a digital negative; and JPEG, the most common, has compressed data. Each has its advocates.

7. Black-and-white photos have a limited audience and are not easily sold. It really didn't matter in the beginning, because it was important for me to initially test what I was putting out to be seen.

8. Respecting what the curator wants and what she thinks will be of interest to her audience is key to collaborating and building relationships critical to receptivity and to the enthusiasm of others.

9. I'm still not sure that Ansel Adams started this way.

CHAPTER THREE

My First Course

Thankfully, when I started taking photos in 2004, there were already point-and-shoot digital cameras that did a lot of the work for me. As the cameras got more and more sophisticated, the easier they were to use out of the box, and they were very forgiving. Post-production changes became possible without the detailed work that Photoshop would have required of me. And, I had Troy as a backup. I knew from the beginning that I wasn't going to become a photographer by enrollment in professional, formal training. Nearing my seventy-fifth birthday, it wasn't going to be so easy for me to learn much of the science of photography. I didn't fully comprehend when many of my photography friends and acquaintances spoke this strange photographic, mathematical language that I had never been exposed to, nor was I very likely to learn. I didn't know when certain picture-taking techniques were truly needed. I wasn't an angles and lighting person. I just took what I liked. And, sometimes it was more blurred than I'd hoped for.

I had to do better.

Shirley arranged for me to see the gallery director at the Weston Gallery, a leader of vintage and contemporary photography that was located nearby in Carmel, California. Putting together my "portfolio" in a large, black carrying case, practicing my elevator speech, I had just a few minutes to show my work. I realized afterward that the gallery (www.westongallery.com), was one of the most famous repositories of black-and-white photography, specializing in works of Ansel Adams, the Westons (Edward and Brett), Bernice Abbott, and Robert Mapplethorpe, to mention a few!

The director told me that I should apply to peer-reviewed exhibits (see CallforEntry.org) and work toward creating a track record of successful exhibits that would be critical later to increasing acceptance of my work at more established galleries. He recommended taking more courses.

I also read a few how-to books, collected more and more photo books taken by the masters of early black-and-white photography and later artists (5–7,11–17,19,20), and signed up for an online course on street photography.

It was a four-week course, offered by the Perfect Picture School of Photography, (PPSOP), with assigned reading, but mostly required taking pictures on location, uploading them and getting feedback from a distant virtual teacher with whom I would never talk to personally. The assignments each week were to pick a location in San Francisco, spend time on the streets taking photos, selecting my "best" to upload, and wait for feedback from the teacher.

I don't really remember very much about the feedback, but I do remember the direct experiences of spending a few hours on the streets for the next four straight weeks at very different locations.

The locations I chose were meant to be my representative

street photography sites: at 3rd and Montgomery at Market Street, a busy cross-street of commuters on their way to work; at the Ferry Building on the Embarcadero, a tourist destination and crowded transit terminal; on Clement Street, a location on the west side of San Francisco that is a local Chinese commercial center; and finally, the street entrance at the 16th and Mission Street BART station, at that time a human melting pot of workers, wandering transients, and street dwellers.

3rd and Montgomery Street

This was an easy location for me to start because no one was looking at me. There were no other photographers around. Everyone was on his or her way to work, along with a few tourists and occasional street characters looking for handouts or just minding their own business, resting on streets where they had spent the night. During the weekday, it reminded me of a busy Manhattan street corner, where the speed and destination-intent walking precluded any human contact. Cell phones and I-pods plugged into ears distanced interaction between people even further.

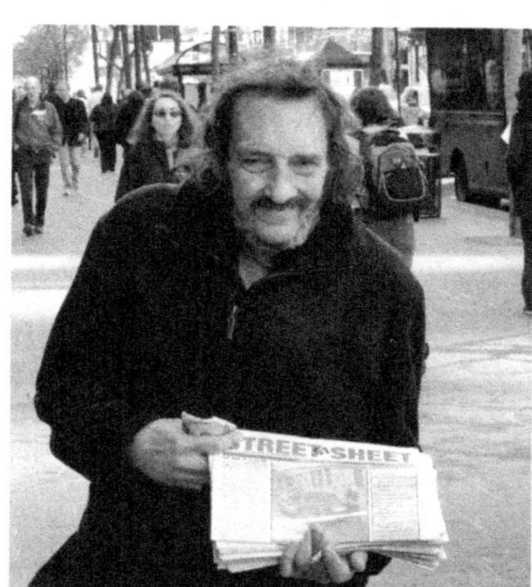
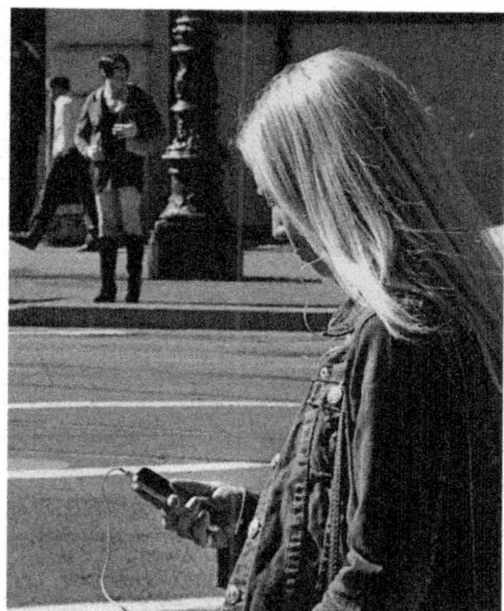

3rd and Montgomery Streets, San Francisco

The Ferry Building

The famous ferry terminal on San Francisco Bay is full of commuters walking to and from their work, tourists and locals buying food, fresh fruit, and veggies at the Farmers Market outside, along with many high-end food stores and tourist booths inside. It was hard not to include people taking photos of one another—pretty boring.

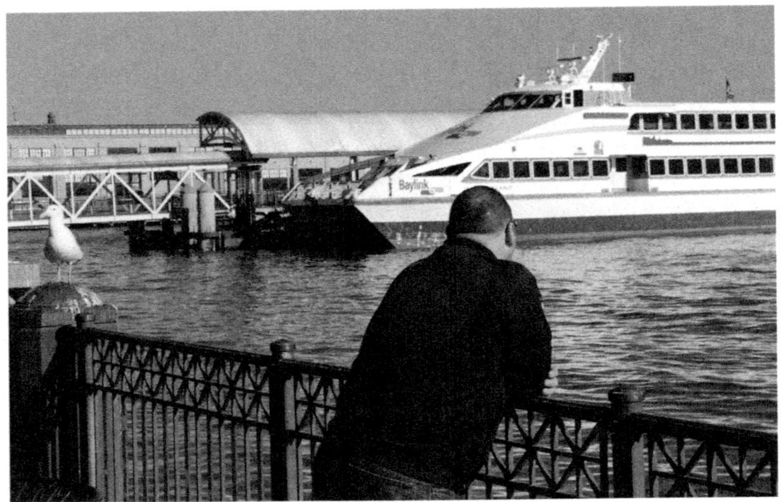

Ferry Building, San Francisco

Clement Street

Clement Street, on the other hand, is a busy, local neighborhood of restaurants, markets, and day-to-day-living shops where a predominantly Chinese population go about their business, expecting everyone to do the same. Not necessarily an unfriendly neighborhood, but not frequented by many tourists nor others without specific reasons.

As mentioned, the first two were relatively easy. The most common reaction to my taking photos on Clement Street, on the other hand, was people looking the other way, covering up their faces, keeping their personal distance, and not infrequently, with palpable hostility. This was definitely not the place to take spontaneous photos, unless they were ones of surprise and distance.

The instructor advised us, if we met any resistance or questioning about what we were doing, to tell them we were taking a photography course. This didn't work on Clement because of language barriers, and they were not that welcoming anyway. Issues such as privacy, respect, dignity for the family, and the important role of lifelong relationships and friendships may have influenced the local response to my wanting to take pictures along the streets. (China.daily.com, 04/04/2015, Cultural differences between China and the US (28))

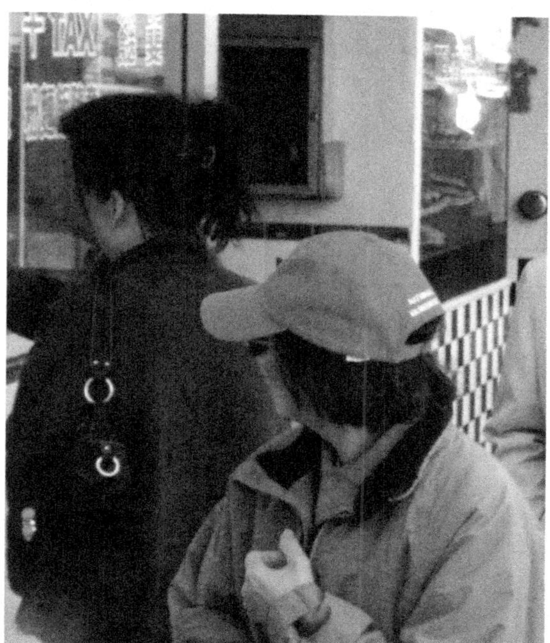

*Clement Street,
San Francisco*

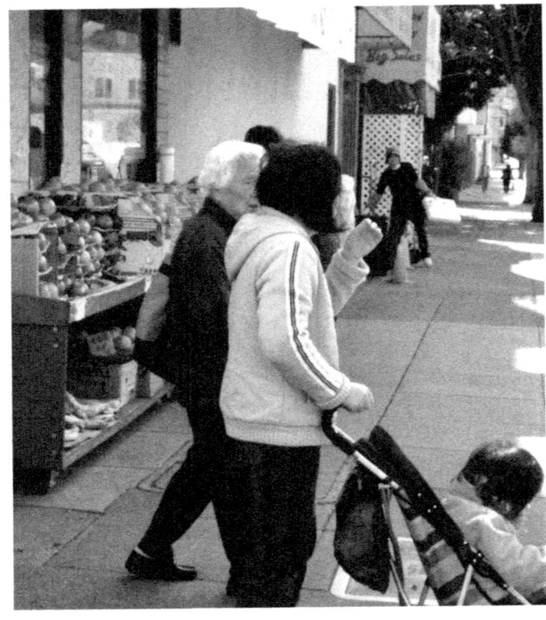

*Clement Street,
San Francisco*

16th and Mission St.

Sixteenth and Mission was the most challenging of all the locations I had selected. This BART station is the temporary daytime street gathering for people living nearby, some looking more or less like they had just been released from jail or a mental health institution, others waiting impatiently for bus or rail transportation, or just hanging out, mixed with workers, families, and the multicultural diversity of San Francisco.

It started out simply enough, taking pictures of people sitting at a nearby bench. The interchange went something like this:

"What are you doing?"

I looked over to a man in a tattered shirt and dirty jeans and smiled my best smile.

Standing up, he repeated loudly, "WHAT ARE YOU DOING?"

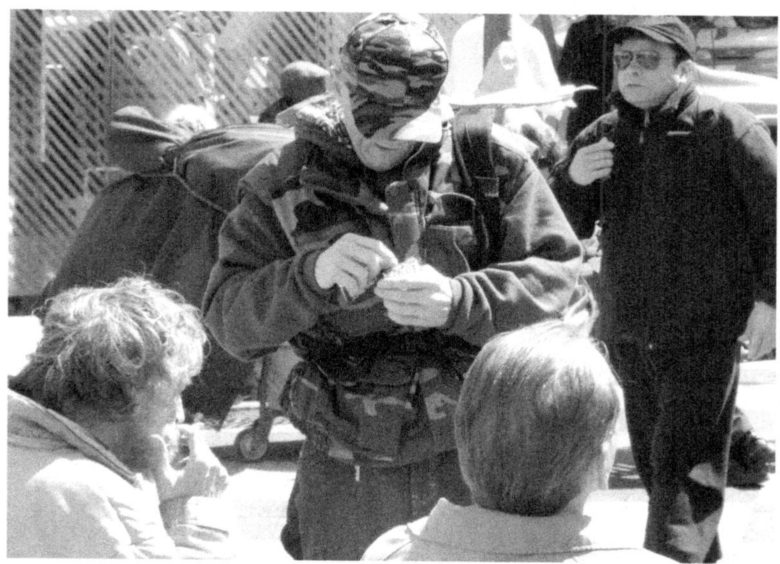

16th and Mission Streets, BART Entrance, San Francisco

I responded with the teacher's advice, "I'm taking a photography class."

He looked at the others sitting close by. He smiled, then frowned, reaching into his pocket and pointing, " Yeah, sure— bet you are with the cops!"

A few more exchanges, followed by my rapid retreat, laughter all around, finger pointing and fist bumping continued.

It didn't get much better. More confrontations followed with similar encounters and I was out of there! I had planned to spend several hours taking pictures. My site visit lasted twenty minutes. And, I considered myself lucky. Never take a camera into a "war zone" unless you are prepared for war, I thought. With my apologies to people whom I didn't understand at the time, and who didn't understand me either.

This street course taught me that cameras mean very different things to different people in our country. I need to have my camera ready, look for photographic moments, keep a look out for myself, and know when to leave hostile territory. Besides the feedback received from the teacher and learning a few of the techniques of street photography, I discovered very quickly there are acceptable and unacceptable standards for proper camera etiquette and proper behavior.

Having one's photo taken by a stranger is not greeted with universal acceptance. There are variable responses depending on culture, social group norms, and by wide individual differences. If there is any question about what you are doing, being polite, asking permission, and making human contact usually leads to positive interactions in most situations. Pointing cameras at people, taking pictures of people with oddities in dress, angry demeanor, and emotional liability states, along with differing cultural norms, raises the hostility level. Common sense makes sense.

What is allowable? There are real concerns about taking pictures without permission, since the laws are not very clear and vary considerably. My online instructor suggested that public spaces are public, thought to be acceptable for taking most photos without formal permission. Commercial intent of their use also makes a difference. Will they be for sale? Do you need to get a release? Seeking permission almost universally leads to posing for pictures. Most of my photos ops until very recently have been spontaneous, my feeling being that posing doesn't lead to very interesting pictures; yet, privacy and respect for people's wishes is an issue. Seeking permission for street photography continues to be unclear.

More learning:

1. Feedback is critical and comes from many sources: from peer review of work submitted for exhibits, from gallery directors, and from people who come to exhibits who don't necessarily like what they see. It is a humbling experience to be given honest and real feedback about one's photos and identifying areas needed for improvement, but so necessary to hear.

2. Gallery owners and others who sell photographs are motivated by the quality of the art, but equally look for the possibility of a potential sale; it is their business.

3. Feedback also comes from the people you photograph. Their reactions to cameras and having their picture taken vary greatly and are part of their individual stories. Seeking permission to take pictures remains controversial with differing views and cultural norms.

4. Professional photography is more than a one-person venture. It takes varying skills and resources to make a career out of it. Asking for help and developing needed resources are essential for learning.

5. Street photography offers an unusual opportunity to see life and experience huge differences in responses to holding a camera. There is no substitute for taking pictures—as many as possible in as many different settings.

SECTION II

Reality

(2011–2015)

CHAPTER FOUR

A Trip to the Sorbonne (2011, 2012)

My photographic radar increases when I get off the plane in Paris. There are so many interesting images of people and places, literally around every corner. Paris is a photographer's dream, always. I come home with a camera full of photos that are beautiful reminders of why we go back every year.

My expectations are that moments are waiting for me there. My strategy is one of opportunity and opportunism. Picture-taking for me becomes an intentional act, but without any planned behavior or expectations. I have an attitude of "I'm here, get ready world." "What's in store today?" "Next?"

Starting by getting the camera ready (see chapter 11), assessing the light, looking at background, I look for unplanned, spontaneous moments and take them. Multiple photos at the same site don't necessarily guarantee results, but digital cameras allow for more than one mistake. They are so forgiving.

Truth is, everything is interesting if you can focus yourself to be in the immediate present as fully as possible. I try to frame the picture and not edit myself or be overly critical while taking pictures, using my intuition to decide when to press the shutter. Sometimes seconds feel like minutes. It doesn't always work, but I am more than likely to successfully capture a moment without fully doing so intentionally.

On one of our trips, a French lawyer friend who had seen my art, asked if I would ever consider having a show in Paris. Having a show in Paris? We started to kid around a bit and I finally said, "Well, maybe you could be my agent." She became very serious, saying "why not?" We talked more about what that might mean and she said she would get back to me.

Months passed; I had forgotten our brief discussion, and then one day I received an email from her. She had found an annual meeting at the Sorbonne for artists from medicine and related medical fields. There was interest in my photos. Could she explore it some more? She had made contact with the curator responsible for the show, shown her some of my work. A few weeks later, I was accepted! Moi? Would I be able to send four photos for a space in the show? It was set for June 5–25, 2011.

The logistics of an international showing are daunting. They require printing and sending photos to Paris as individual archival prints, finding an atelier (a shop or studio of a professional artist in fine arts that prepares high quality work suitable for gallery hanging), then having the photos mounted, framed, and delivered to the show. It also involves setting a price for their sale, having them hanged, finding a shipping resource in France and Europe and sending the unsold pictures back to the U.S. And, it meant traveling to Paris for the opening!

It made no sense to frame pictures in the U.S and ship them over for the show. So, we hand-carried the four prints on the plane and dropped them off at a local atelier in Paris when we went for our usual visit in April, planning to return two months later in June for the opening of the show. The framing was much more expensive than in the U.S., the logistics of framing within the available time a real problem, transportation to the event problematic. The person we had selected didn't seem to understand what I needed and why. Even with language help, the communication difficulties between the shopkeeper and myself continued. After we left his shop that day, it seemed very possible that my exhibit might still fall apart: the logistics seemed insurmountable.

Everything turned out fine, however, our friend carrying the photos herself on the Metro from the atelier to the Sorbonne. We arrived in Paris a few days before opening night, and arranged to be at the location with our "agent" for the hanging of my four pictures. She introduced us to the organizer of the exhibit, proud as we were and beaming as we walked along the hallway to the spot that had been selected. We pointed to a better location and she agreed. For me, it was also a huge challenge to think about preparing for a very different audience. How would they react to photos taken in Paris by an American?

More than five hundred people came to the opening that evening, a jazz band played, champagne and canapés were on hand, and the crowd seemed excited to see the work from more than one hundred fifty artists who had been selected that year. Not speaking French, it was hard to imagine communicating with anyone who might stop and ask a question about my work. Iris had offered to translate, but I said let's try and see what happens with just me.

Viewers walked through the crowded hall looking at exhibits on both sides, randomly scanning for something of interest. People would glance over, suddenly stop at my exhibit, look again and then move in for a much closer look. "Ah, Cartier-Bresson?" they said. They looked at me and smiled when I said "Oui!" They smiled, looked again and said "Oui!" They approached even closer, looking up and down, spending even more time; and finally, "Je vous en remercie!" Thank you, I translated, tears forming in my eyes.

These interchanges happened several times that evening whenever my work connected. We were communicating via pictures without having to say a word. It was true again the following year when I returned to Paris for a second exhibit. I sold three photos that first year. (A couple from Lausanne bought the picture of the old man, and a psychiatrist, the two older women crossing the street.) The atelier, by the way, greeted me in 2012 with a warm smile, a handshake and a promise to take the latest framed pictures to the show himself.

My main conclusion from these exhibits was that there is a French audience that does understand what I am trying to do and appreciates my attempts to honor and share their way of life. Every year we go, it becomes harder and harder not to want to find a Parisian gallery interested in showing my work, spend even more time in Paris, learn French, and become more immersed in the photography scene there. It still remains a dream, something that might happen one day.

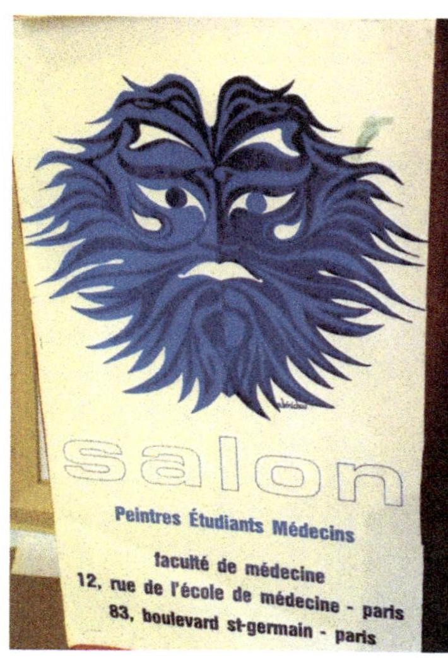

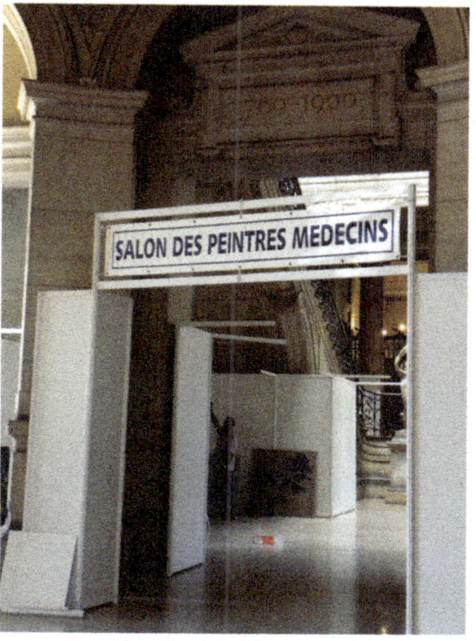

Paris (IV) The Sorbonne

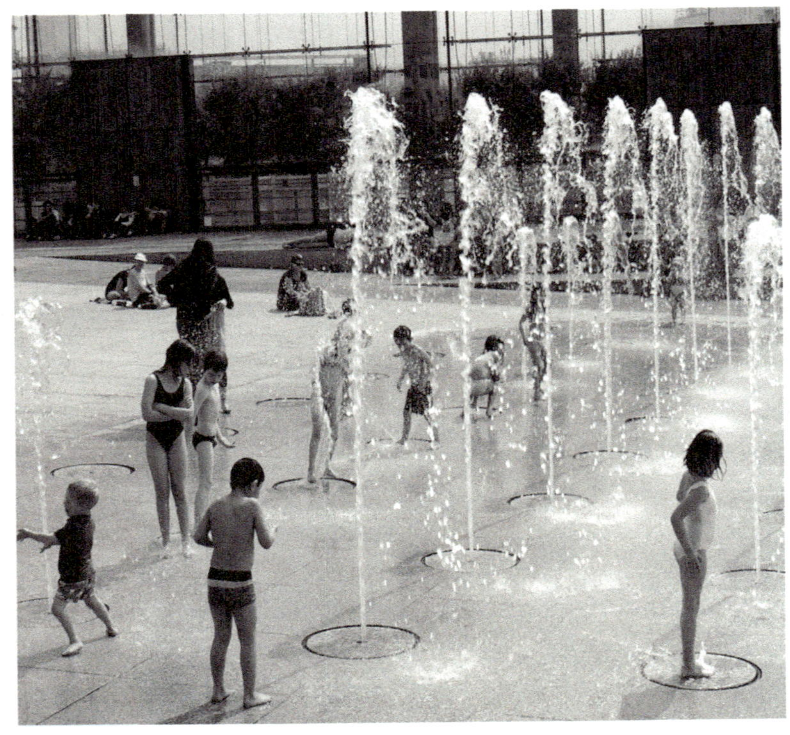

Citroen Park, Paris

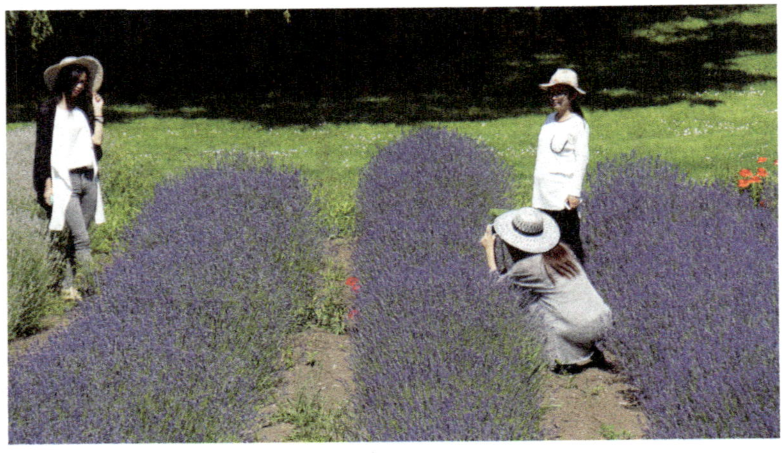

Looks like Provence, but it's Sequim, WA

CHAPTER FIVE

It Wasn't That Simple

Reality hit hard following the second exhibit at the Sorbonne the summer of 2012.

I realized that I really didn't know what to do next. An exhibit in New York? Another, back in Paris? Look for galleries to represent and sell my work? Reach out to a museum?

My fantasy was that a story would soon be written in the English language edition of LeMonde (with apologies):

> *"Retired American doctor, now living with his wife in Paris, holds another successful one-person exhibit. French premier attends along with the U.S. ambassador...."*

It didn't happen that way. We came back from Paris the summer of 2012, my eyes gleaming, waiting to be discovered. The reality, at that moment, was that I was still a retired physician, like so many wannabes, producing black-and-white pictures of Paris. That was it.

I stayed busy: revised People I've Seen II in October 2012 and

published a new book, Children I've Seen, in the fall of 2012.
I was accepted for two more juried shows submitting photos
through Café Management: a photo was accepted in Louisville,
Colorado, for the Potter (see page 30), at the 21st Annual
Louisville National Juried Photography Show in 2012; and the
following year, another exhibit in August of 2013 for Friends (see
page 37), at the 4th International Juried Exhibition in Tieton,
Washington.

What followed were a series of efforts, submitting to various
juried shows in the U.S., followed by a stream of responses:
"Thank you, but we had so many 'qualified' artists this year, we
couldn't take them all." Over the next few years, I sent in eight
applications that were not invited.

I am not sure entirely why or how, but my career slowed.
Honestly, I think it had to do with a lack of better marketing, not
having a plan of what to do next, needing to reach out, network
and make more contacts, and most importantly, having a clear
direction. It didn't help that I was beginning to have problems
walking and standing.

I had to acquire new and different photography skills, while
realistically accepting that I was becoming less physically
active; and yet, I had to become much more proactive. And,
I needed more personal work to discover what was missing
as a photographer. I had lost my focus—very bad for a
photographer.

CHAPTER SIX

What Is My Passion?

By 2009 I had already begun to explore possible alternatives to black-and-white photos. At a Manet exhibit at the D'Orsay Museum in Paris, the docent had pointed out that he had sold many small still-life paintings of fruit and vegetables in order to pay his bills. He was not able to find a market place for his larger impressionist paintings; like many artists he struggled to survive, well before he was recognized as one of the world's greatest artists.

Calendars

Publishing an annual calendar, using Shutterfly, became my "still lifes." I didn't sell them, but they quickly became a popular way of sharing my work with those who were interested. Abstract photos—"funny-angle photography" is what I called them—were not meant to be, nor would they ever be perceived to be pictures of life-changing moments. Having no profound meaning in mind, they were photos for fun, not meant to be emotionally laden works.

Now in their seventh year (2010–), these pleasing visuals are easy to look at every calendar day of the month. Soon, I was sending more than seventy-five complimentary calendars to family, friends, and others interested in my work. Starting with the familiar black and whites already seen in my earlier books and exhibits, I added colorful landscapes and abstract photos such as pictures of food preparation (see mango ice cream, soufflé, and pumpkins). Japanese maples and umbrellas, Christmas ornaments and gingko leaves, were ways to show design elements suitable for calendars. Emails and phone calls start every year in August, asking when next year's calendars are going to arrive.

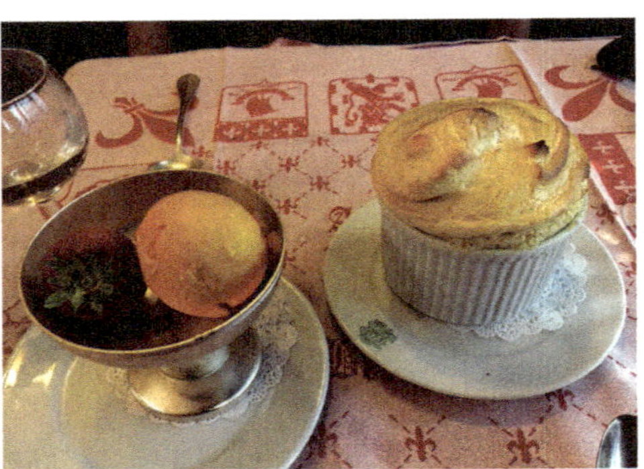

7th Arrondessement, Paris

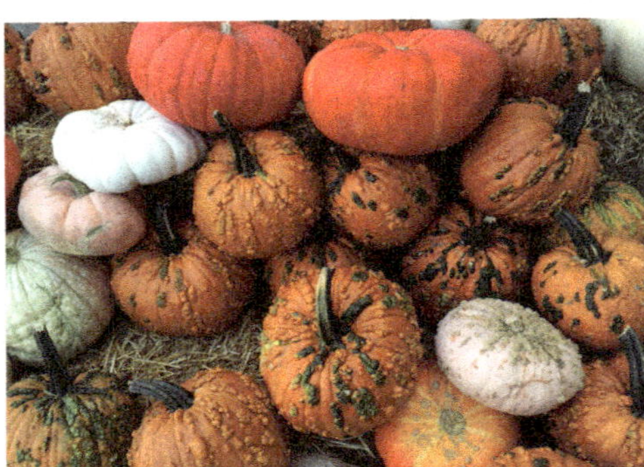

Canby, Oregon

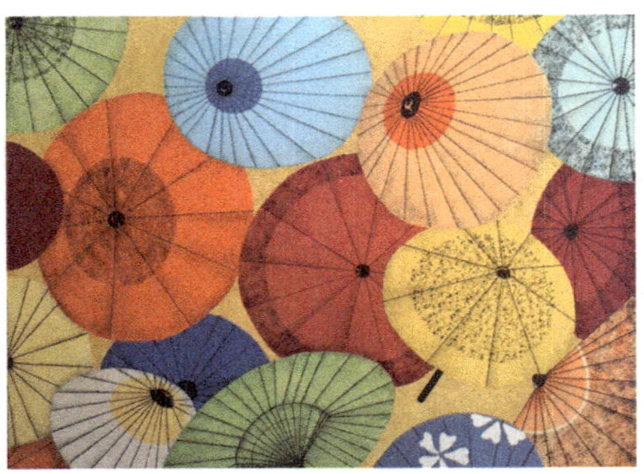

Japantown, San Francisco

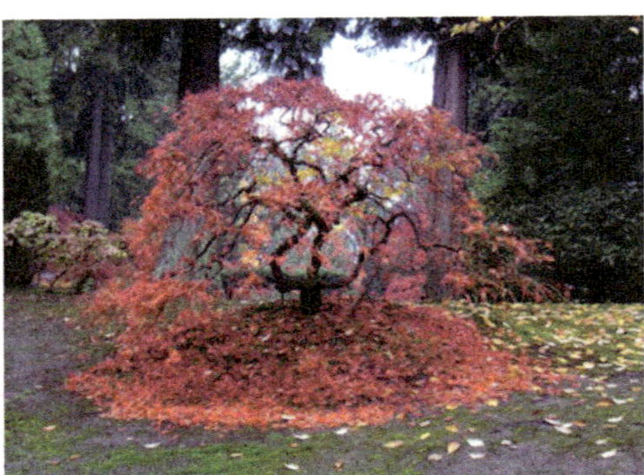

Portland Japanese Gardens

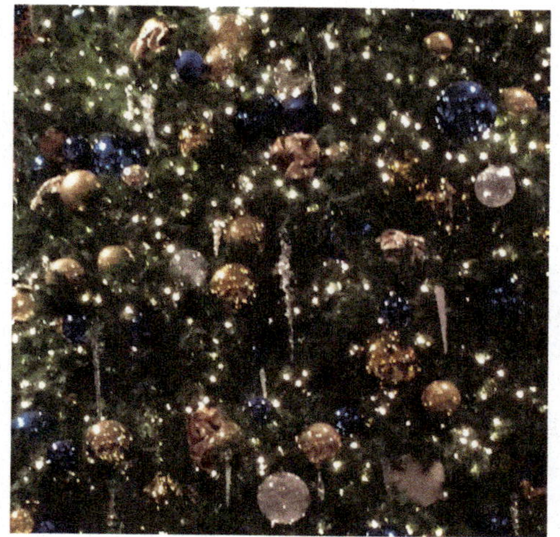

Nob Hill, SF Fairmont Hotel

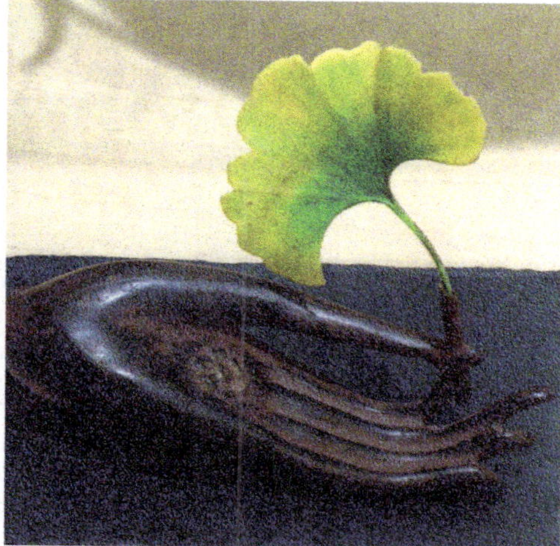

South Park, San Francisco

Multimedia

When Iris, not only a fine medical doctor and academic at Stanford, but also a fused-glass artist, asked if she might pair some of my abstract photos with newly created glass art, we started a collaborative multimedia series. Her idea was to show photos and their complementary fused glass pieces side-by-side as a matched pair, emphasizing similarities in design and also illustrating differing media. Visions en Verre, Glass Visions, was accepted for a joint exhibit at the Carmel Valley glass art studio of Alan Masaoka in August 2012; and again, as part of a juried show at Stanford from September 2013 to June 2014. Well received, we celebrated our collaboration and shared experience, sold a few of the paired works from the exhibit, and planned to work together again on similar efforts in the future.

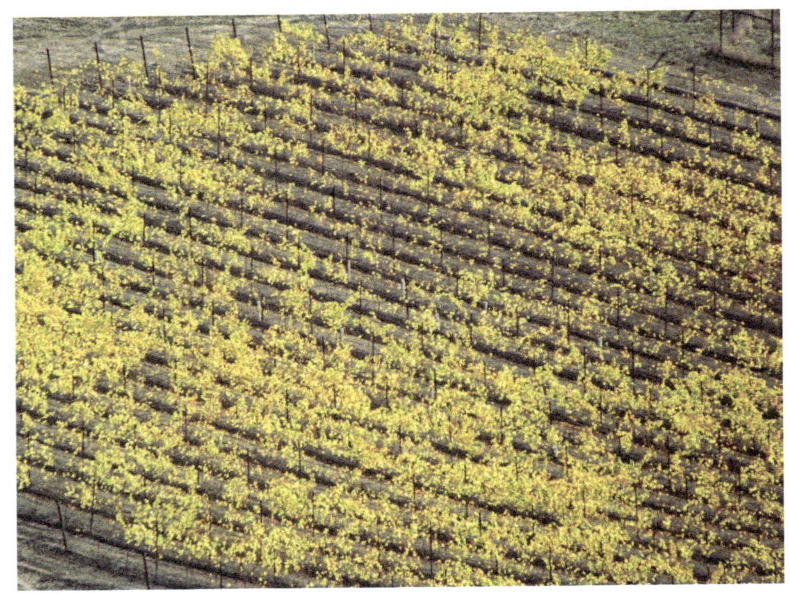

The original photo, Carmel Valley, California

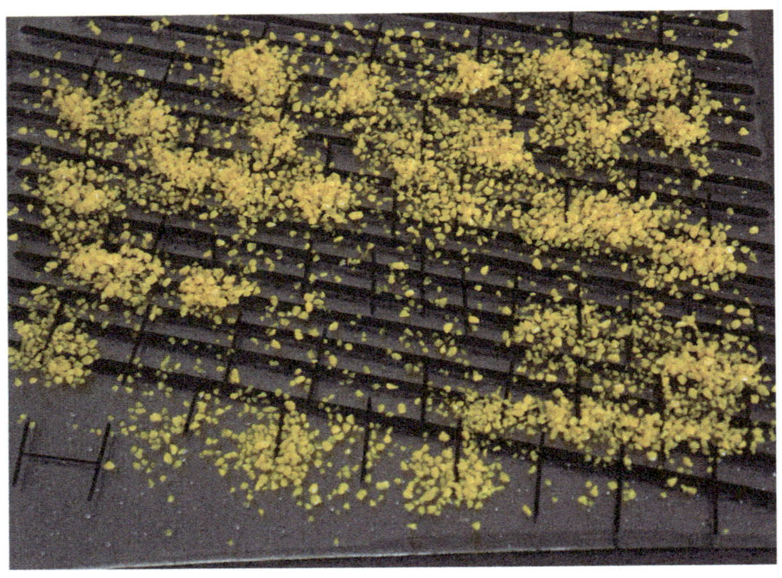

Fused-Glass Design

Real life had also intervened. I was nearing eighty, bones and joints starting to creak, conditions appeared that didn't go away, and I became aware that I was going to have physical limitations on what I could do. The doctors said I had spinal stenosis, a condition of the skeletal spine pressing on the nerve roots that could soon keep me from walking distances and standing for long periods of time. We started to plan to move from a daily routine of climbing stairs to reach our place and walking everywhere in San Francisco and began searching for a home on a single floor. Physical therapy helped and a cardiac program using a stationary bicycle kept me in shape. I needed to think about what might realistically be called the art of what's possible.

I keep coming back to Shirley's earlier question: What is my passion?

Despite the limited responses to my black-and-white photography, it has continued to be my primary way of artistic expression. I love its texture and subtlety, the shadows and shades of gray without the added "distraction" of color, the way it pulls me in, wanting to be a part of the scene. The French viewers at the exhibits in Paris, the personal dialogue and positive feedback over the years from many people and the very different audiences at the exhibits, the satisfaction when chosen for an exhibit—how it makes me feel—were critical signposts helping me to decide.

I continue to question how best to improve my art. I do not want to be limited to only one way of presentation, i.e., to be "monochromatic." Using color and abstract photography and other approaches such as the production of calendars, pairings with other media such as glass, are additional ways to express myself. Photography is my ongoing experiment; and it should be.

I also want to find ways to reach a larger audience for the black and whites. Perhaps further self-publication and better

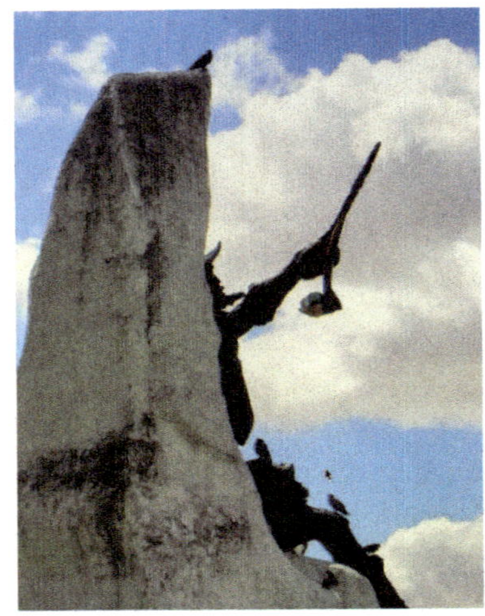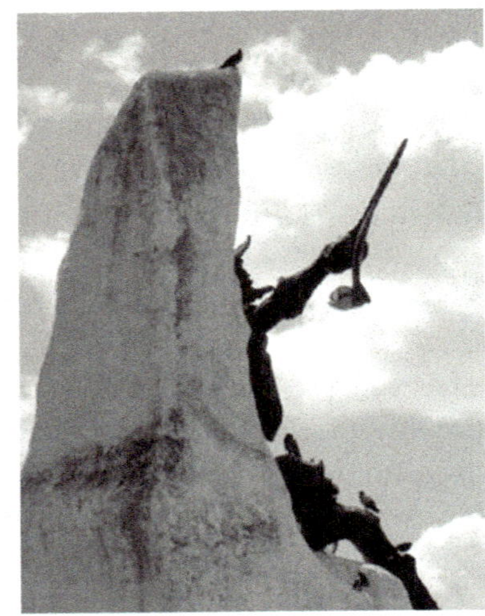

Buenos Aires, Argentina

marketing are ways to connect with a larger audience. And, the question still remains: how do I measure success?

My website (www.dalegarellphotography.com) is updated annually and I continue to consider alternatives such as self-publishing, working again with an agent, and submitting my work for juried shows.

I have accepted that not everyone likes my work; many want more color, action, beauty, or scenes of world breaking events. My pictures were still blurred, cropped; and to a critical and knowledgeable eye, many have said that was hardly of professional quality.

The realities of my photography and my life:

1) Not having a plan has made me wander back and forth, looking for other possibilities to take photos and show my work, questioning my direction and accept that I wasn't focused.

2) I discovered I can create lots of different things, but it is not enough to satisfy my dreams and hopes of using black-and-white photography as my primary medium.

3) On the other hand, I have fun with these new efforts; maybe it was time to stop the more serious ones.

4) I need to be less self-impressed and more humble.

5) I need to focus on more than my camera; my aging was beginning to get in the way.

SECTION III

Becoming a Photographer

(2015)

CHAPTER SEVEN

Paris Revisited

found it ironic. Just at the time I was floundering, questioning my art and whether I might ever become a serious photographer, I learned about a course in photojournalism offered by Peter Turnley in Paris during the first week in July of 2015 (peterturnley.com). Peter is an internationally recognized photographer and spends half the year in Paris at his studio in the Marais and the other half in Harlem in New York City. He has worked for Newsweek for decades and taken live action photos from many of the hotspots in the world. He has also published his photographs of Paris and knows the city intimately (30). He worked with Cartier-Bresson's master printer, Voja Mitrovic, learning techniques of silver gelatin printing. (We were so pleased to meet Voya who shared examples of Cartier-Bresson's photos with our class.)

Our weeklong assignment was to photograph the streets of Paris, using a wide-angle lens, and bring the photos back to class the next day where we would review each other's work under Peter's guidance. Our discussions were open, full of interaction, and fueled by the excitement of taking and talking about our own photos, sharing much in common.

Day one was stressful, but relatively easy. Crossing the street on the left bank of the Seine was a large group of participants from a church nearby, bride and groom hand-in-hand, accompanied by their wedding photographer. I got shots of the bride and groom with the new wide angle, changed them into black and white, and returned the next day for Peter and our class to review. Peter was kind, but firm. He said, "Dale, these are really good photos, but—(I waited)—do you see where the photographer is in the picture, and the bridal party? I want you to be somewhere in between, capturing the newlyweds, as close as you can get!"

He had to be kidding. There was no way I could take that kind of picture without being in the picture myself. How could I do that without introducing myself, crashing the wedding, and taking shots without getting their permission? How indeed?

As teachers in medical school, we are encouraged to look for the teachable moment, a time when the medical student or resident is most available and ready to learn something new. It usually is a time when previously held assumptions are questioned—when a person is vulnerable and suddenly open, although not fully aware nor ready to learn something very new. It becomes an opportunity to listen, see the world differently, and consider the possibilities of accepting new ideas about themselves and their actions.

That was the case for me in Paris that week. I was not going to be able to use my telephoto lens to get close-ups. I was being asked to be in the picture, engage the subject, introduce myself, spend time and listen to what was being said by the people I was photographing.

Day two was a disaster. Suddenly, subjects and situations seemed stale and no longer worth photographing. Everything

I saw was another "ordinary" scene, just like the ones I had previously taken. I walked the streets looking for special moments, not seeing any. All of my earlier assumptions about Paris being one photo opportunity after another were wrong: photo "opportunities" became routine, not worth taking, nor even taking the time to look for them.

I finally found an exit from the Metro and stationed myself at the top of the stairs, waiting. The moments never came or so I thought. I began to wonder—maybe my ability to find a special scene of people experiencing every day life in Paris was never there in the first place. I knew I was being hard on myself. I minimalized my earlier work as not having much substance. If I had hoped that my photos would tell a story, I was not finding much. It was boring. I was boring.

The photos I had been taking were missing something—me. My usual technique was an almost exclusive use of a telephoto lens, cropping the picture until I got as much detail as I could from the artificial close-ups, and cutting out a lot of the interesting details in the process. I began calling myself a "share cropper" (i.e., someone who cropped photos from a distance and shared his results).

I started an internal conversation with my "old self":

"I know that you are having a hard time with all of this," my new self began.

"By approaching our subjects and asking for permission, people might agree to have their picture taken, but not without looking directly at the camera," my old self said.

"Posing is a learned response based on all the pictures taken of us by our families and others," I said, wanting to keep the conversation going. "I understand."

"They look posed; they're not spontaneous. They reduce opportunities to capture that special moment we have been talking about. And besides, why should I change?" my old self went on.

"You're justifying using a telephoto lens," I tried. And, "You are losing all the details of their life around them by cropping, something that you say you want to show to others."

"I know you're right," my old self said.

"You do not realize the distance you unconsciously create from the people we are taking pictures of," my new self continued.

"Sometimes it is not possible to get a close-up.," I realized I was looking for other reasons to continue my old routines.

"But, it doesn't take the place of human interaction. " "Why don't you give it a try?" I concluded.

"I'll think about it."

On the third day, Iris had gone inside a store in the Marais, and I was out on the streets feeling sorry for myself. I saw a young boy, maybe twelve or so, in a wheelchair being pushed by his father. Crossing the street, finally catching up with them, I approached, nervous, depressed, and yet ready to give it a try. It seemed I had no choice.

It turned out they were from Norway, spoke perfect English, and were visiting Paris on holiday. The father told me they were out walking while the rest of the family was shopping. His son never spoke. What follows are a series of consecutive photos and our conversation together:

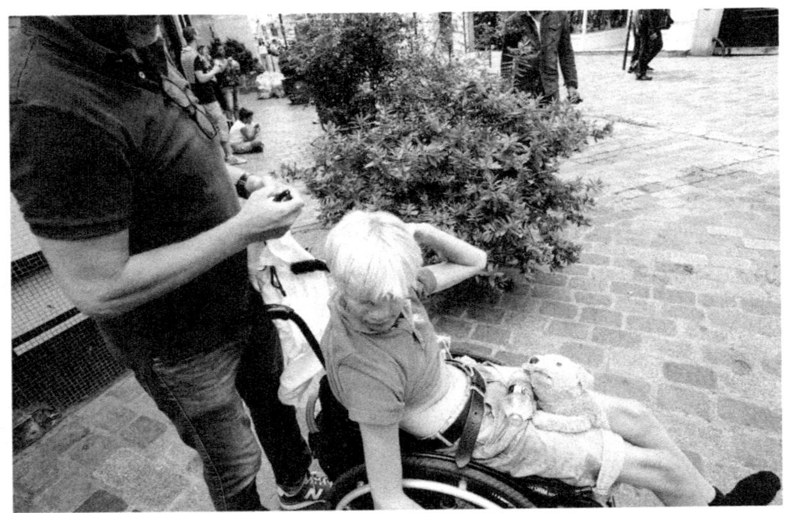

Marais, Paris

My name is Dale. Do you speak English?"

"Yes, we are visiting from Norway."

"What is your son's name?"

"Jon," his father said.

"I am taking a photography class. Is it okay to take a picture of you and your son?"

"Sure."

Picture taken (above).

"Can you ask him if it is okay for me to take his picture, too?" acknowledging I had already done so.

"Is it okay?" the father asked.

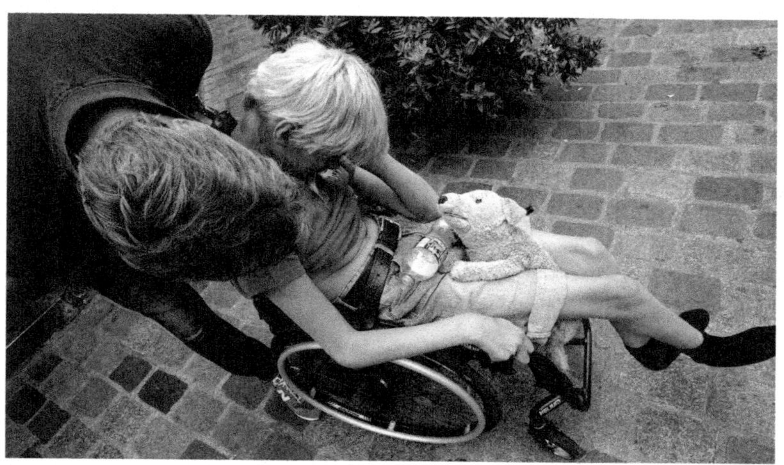

Jon clearly had refused to have his picture taken.

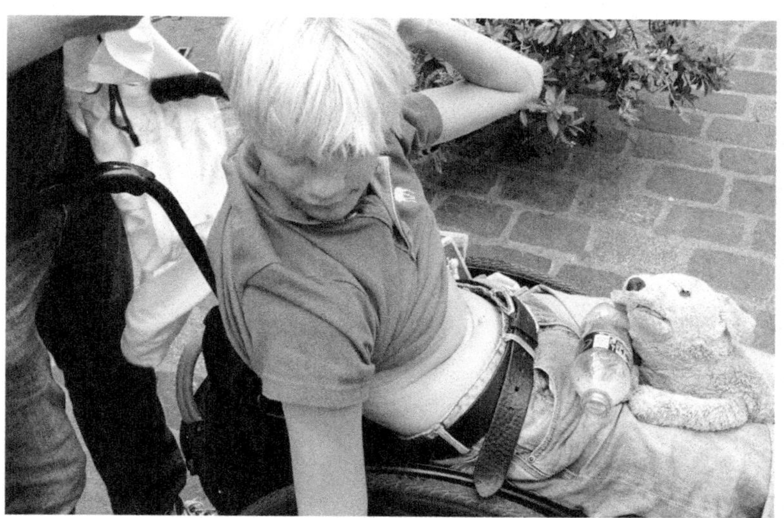

He didn't say it, but I imagined him saying, "GO AWAY!"

At this point, I would have usually backed off, taking "no" as his final answer and that would have been that. I started to leave.

"Would you like to take my picture?" I said suddenly, handing him my camera. He looked up at me from his wheelchair with a big question mark on his face.

His father helped him hold onto the camera initially. He looked through the viewfinder, and Jon pointed and shot his first picture. Then another.

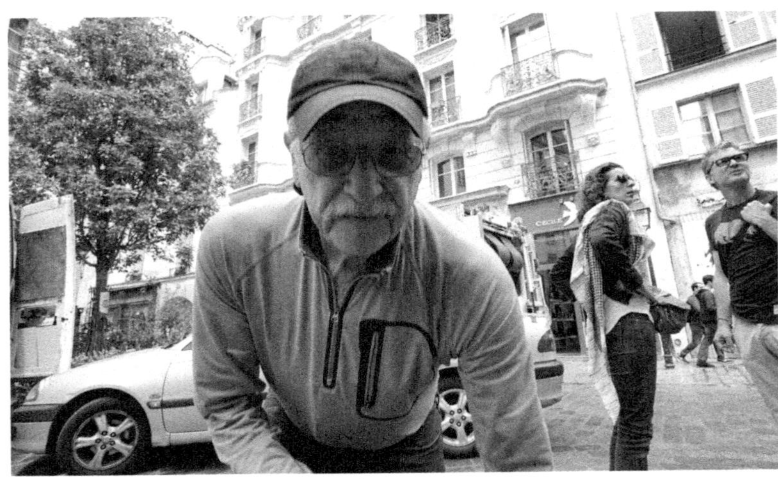

Jon takes his first photo.

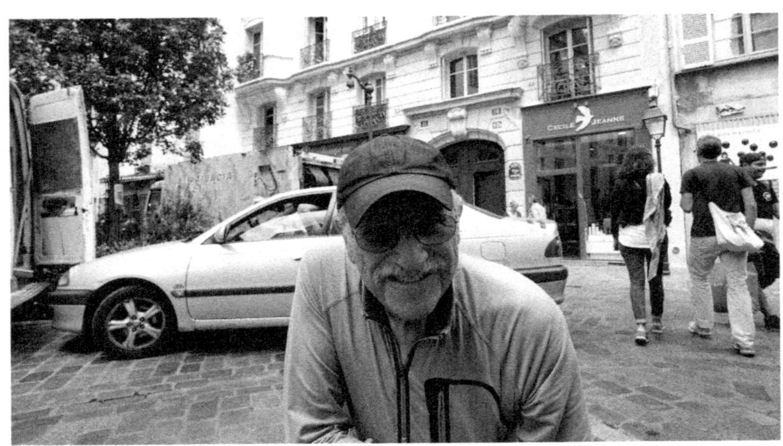

Jon's second photo.

He reached out to give me back the camera. I sat down on the pavement and started to shoot.

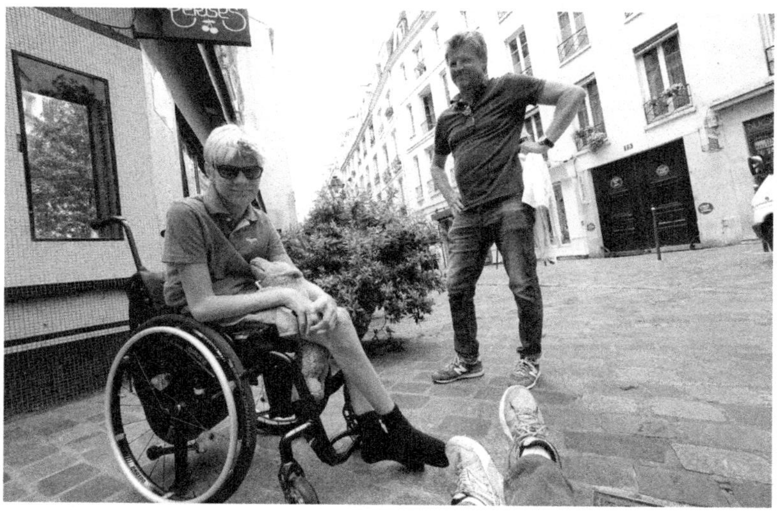

I get the okay (those are my feet).

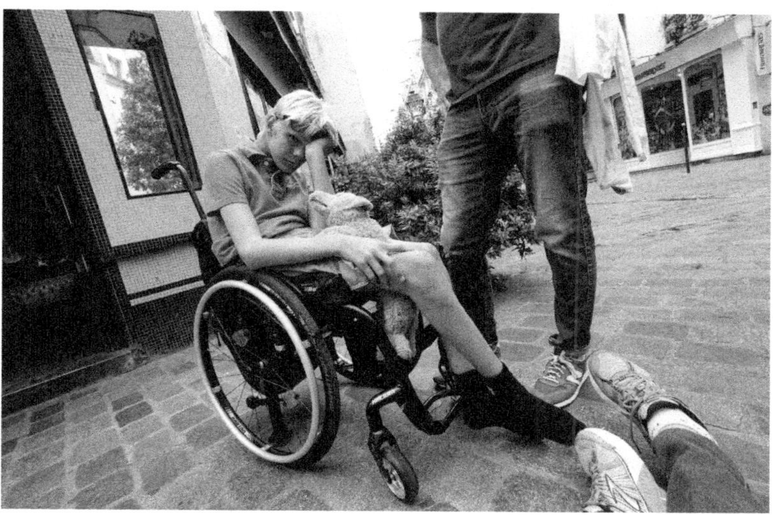

I am sure he was checking me out.

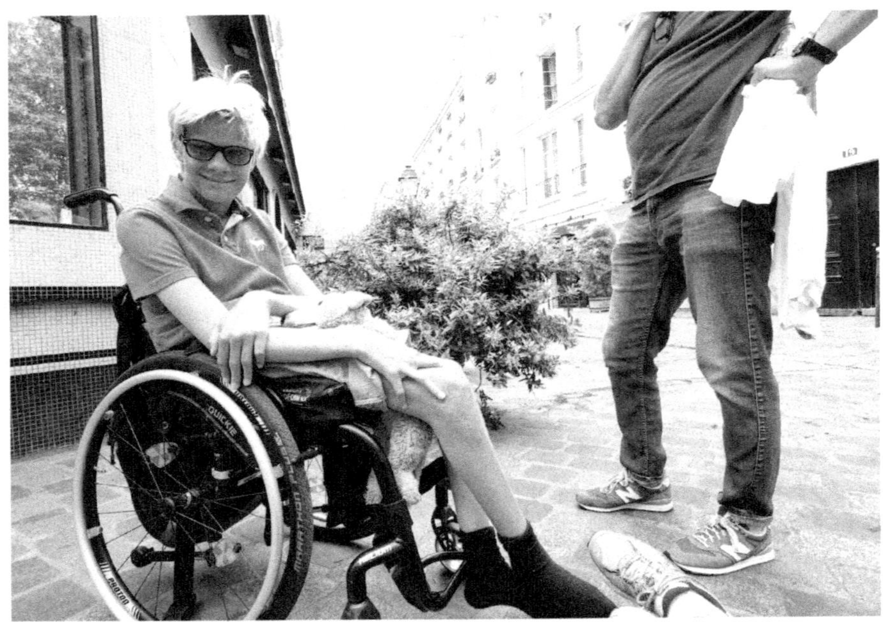

A smile!

I asked Jon if he wanted to take a picture of his father. Not waiting for an answer, I reached over and handed him the camera once again.

I showed him the picture of his dad. He handed me the camera and I took a few more.

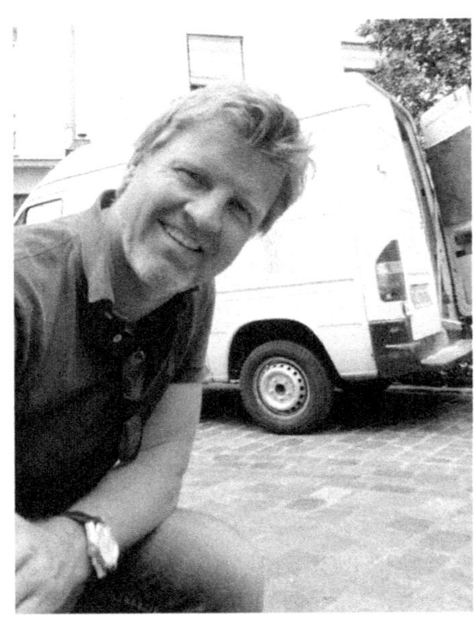

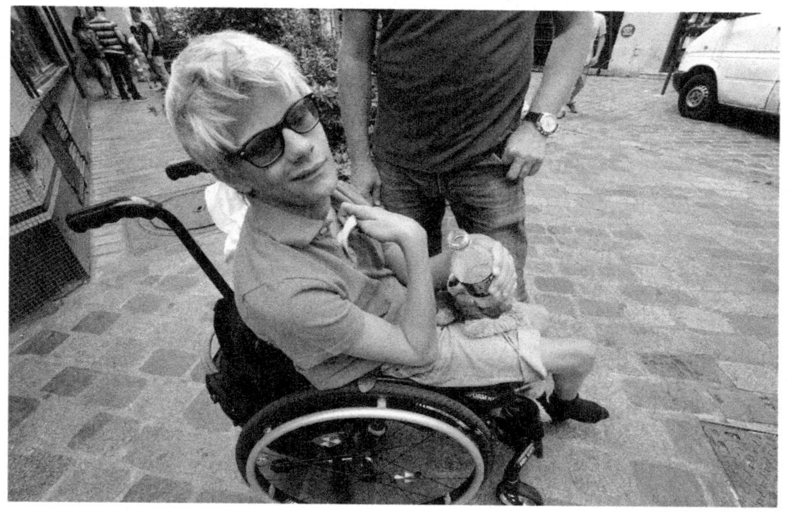

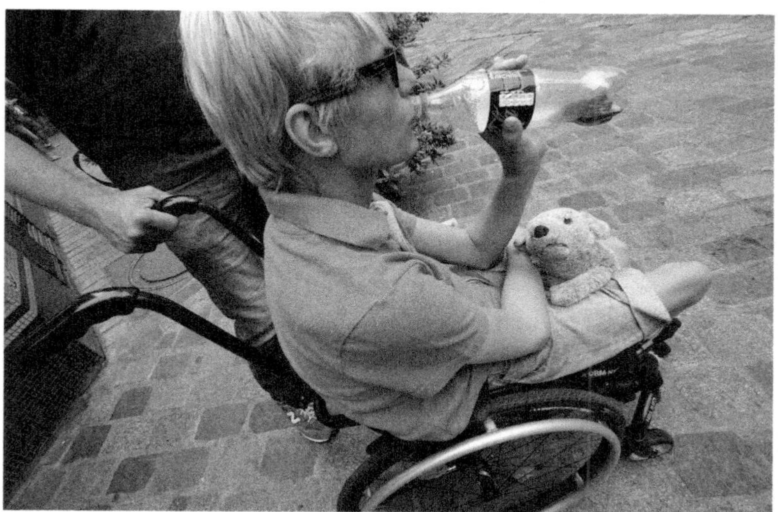

It was over. Jon asked his father for another soda.

I gave them both my card and told them they could contact me if they wanted me to send the photos. (I've never heard from them.)

Walking back across the street, smiling, there were tears in my eyes. Is that how it's done? I had been missing so much.

Later, Peter added: "Most importantly—start thinking like one, act like one, and believe—*become* a photographer."

CHAPTER EIGHT

Photos of People
I Would Have Liked to Talk To

Like everyone, there are lots of photos I have missed, that split second of Cartier-Bresson lost, never to be relived or photographed. Photojournalism has a lot of that. "If only" moments—the ones that got away.

They seem to fall into categories for me: The camera not being ready; having poor reaction time; composition failures; technical meltdowns of the moment; or when the person being photographed suddenly moves in the opposite direction or changes mood.

Others are more related to my own readiness—and this is overcome by emotional deep breathing, creating a rhythm, forgetting everything else, and getting into a groove that permits greater opportunities to focus. These are automatic settings of the mind possible through experience, self-familiarity, and removing or minimalizing the noise of the moment.

The technical part of taking pictures is, by comparison, relatively easy work to accomplish. Digital cameras and their rapid response time help a lot. Composition is something learned though courses and experience. But taking off the "emotional" lens cap requires a different preparation. Techniques can be achieved to settle the mind and reduce outside stresses or those of the moment. By becoming aware of bad photos days, for example, difficulties in internal focusing can be minimized, though our abilities to manage them are not always successful.

Athletes talk about it: When time stops or so it seems. When the quarterback is no longer aware of being on the field, no longer hearing the noise of the crowd on the sidelines. Becoming clear, clearer than they have been. When the football is lighter and anything is possible and the receivers downfield are linked with the quarterback. Pass thrown, caught, and then it's over. Getting into that kind of groove can be a photographic experience as well.

Preparation is not only key to taking meaningful pictures, but I've found pictures themselves continue to have meaning for me beyond the moment when they are taken. Below are a few photos that I have looked back on and later wondered what people might have told me about themselves had I asked them.

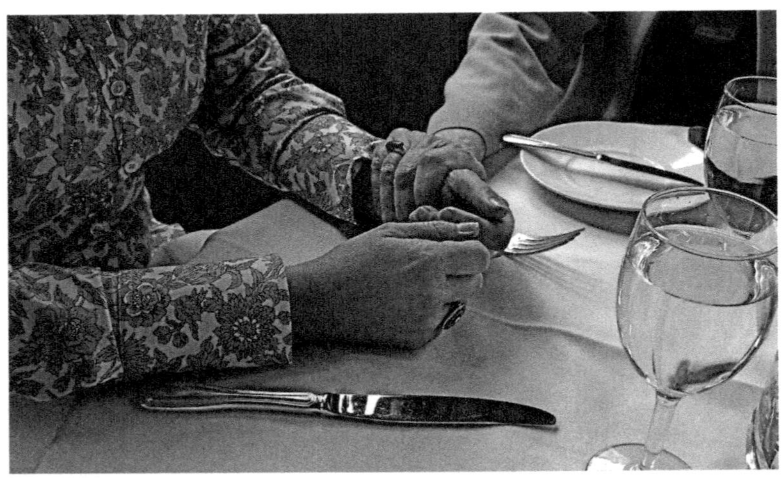

New York City, NY

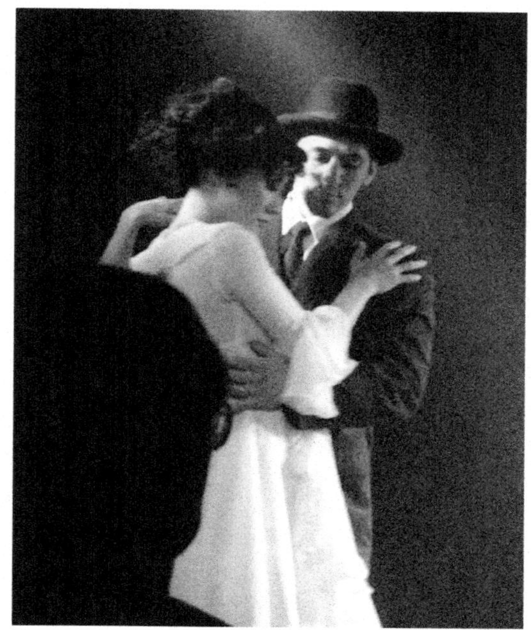

Buenos Aires

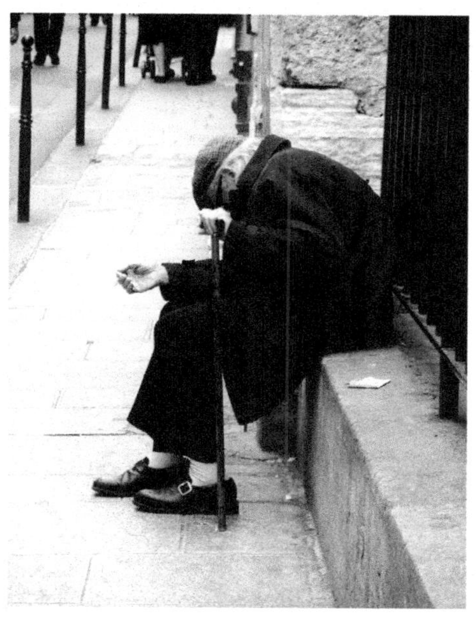

Paris

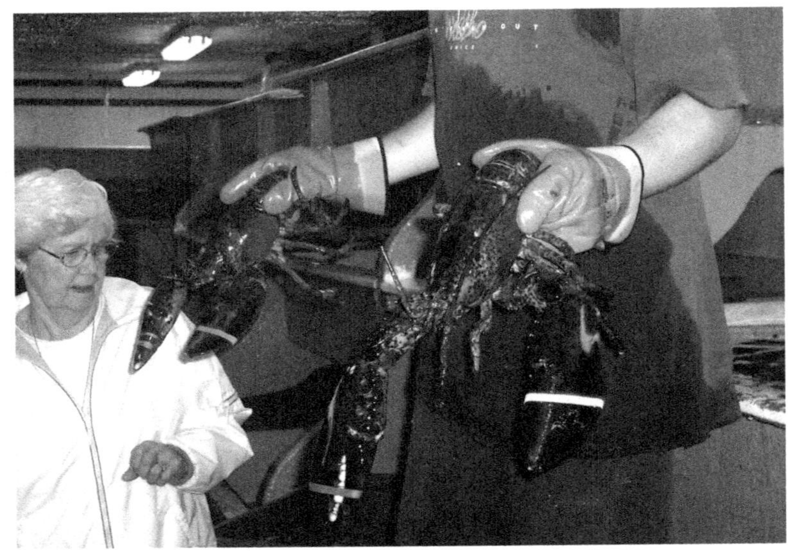

Prince Edward Island, Canada

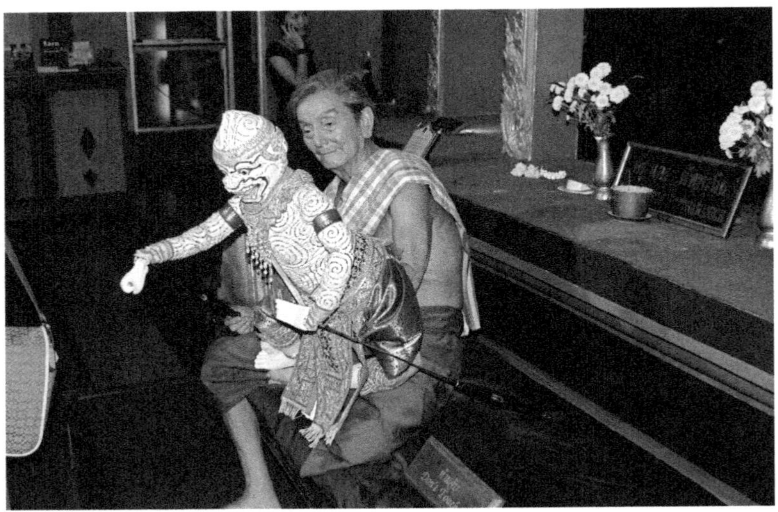

Bangkok, Thailand

They still talk to me.

CHAPTER NINE

Aging Photographer

I belong to the *new* old-age group, the most rapidly growing segment of our population in the U.S. We are more vibrant and alive, with a whole new set of expectations: Some of us are octogenarians who can swim long distances, and still others become marathoners; we start successful careers; make new bucket lists because we finish old ones; seek romance more than companionship; and aspire to write the great American novel. We dream about things we never thought we could or would ever do. We expect to live younger than we are, and we are healthier and more active than ever before.

Many of us refuse to live waiting to die. We mostly accept our futures even when the reality of dying becomes more immediate and even imminent. We know we won't live forever; yet, as a group, we are probably history's most optimistic seniors. We want more and expect more! We have nothing in common with what it was like when our parents reached their eighth or ninth decade. We live in the present rather than the past, accepting our ultimate future without being paralyzed by the fear of it; we think about the possibilities, dream, and then search for ways to

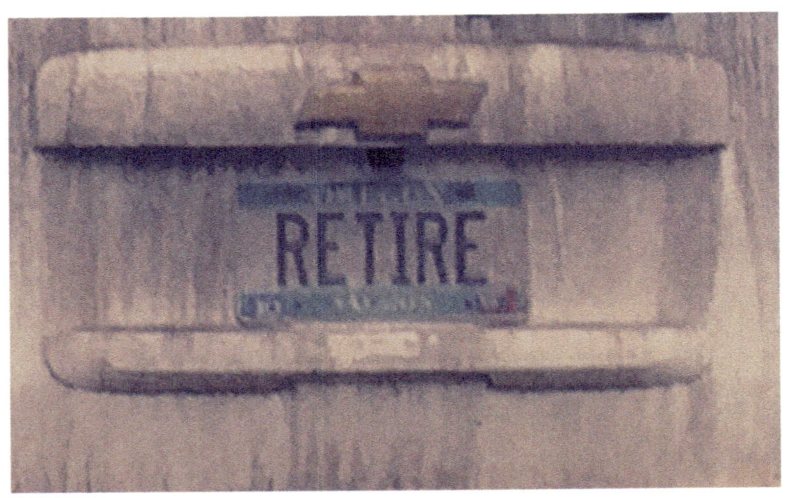

Portland, Oregon

make it happen while facing the physical, mental, psychological, and economic realities of living longer lives.

These are, of course, on my short list of personal challenges for the twenty-first century. I dread getting Alzheimer's or having a fall that limits my mobility. I grieve when loved ones and friends pass away and dread when the time might come when my children may think it is time for me to be "safer," less active, and more the way they remember their grandparents. Why don't I act my age? My answer is I don't want to! Most of the time.

I try to stay a little ahead of what others think I should be doing and continue to test the limits of growing old. I believe my life should be one of discovery and awe, learning and insight, acceptance and recognition, laughter and joy, sadness and recovery, a reaffirmation of beliefs while searching for my own personal wisdom.

But, I can no longer ignore aging completely. Like most of us, I reject lifestyles that involve assisted living and senior citizen settings, and delay even the thought of going to a nursing home. I just don't perceive myself as old. These days, my own aging occurs right in front of me and reminds me that soon the time might come when I will no longer be an active participant and will have to really slow down.

There are, however, some practical changes that have to be made. It will not be possible to take photographs like I used to. But, I will try.

SECTION IV

A Search for
a Photography of the self
(2015-)

CHAPTER TEN

The Camera as a Tool for self-reflection

Wearing a backpack, wheeling luggage, and carrying a cane and camera made it no longer possible for me to negotiate busy airports. Even after checking luggage, and with Iris helping, I was unable to comfortably manage the unpredictability of foreign travel. I was determined to stand and walk as much as possible. I had to accept that I needed help to make the long journey to Paris the summer of 2015.

We called the airline and arranged for a wheelchair and service assistant to meet us at the ticket counter in Portland. When we arrived that day, an elderly lady greeted us; she looked like she might have needed a wheelchair herself! I got into my chair, our helper cracking "why did the chicken?" jokes. She helped us quickly pass through security and passport checks, down back elevators, and finally dropped us off at our gate. We laughed, thanked her, and gave her a tip. She said goodbye with a smile, a final joke, and said she would see us when we returned. I think she really meant it. I didn't take her picture, but I should have.

While waiting to board, I recalled a picture of a little girl in September of 2010 taken from my seat at a wedding in Normandy. What did she see and experience at her level? And then I thought, why not? Take pictures from her view of the world while traveling along in a wheelchair!

The familiar announcement was made: "People who need a little more time for boarding may board first." We walked onto the plane, Iris holding my blue handicapped parking plaque. When we arrived in Seattle, another attendant with my wheelchair greeted us. We were taken along the usual corridors, moving through security and passport control without waiting in long lines. We saw passengers walking hurriedly to catch a flight, or on their way out of the airport, and suddenly we were getting into elevators others wished they could take, traveling by light rail to the international terminal, up another elevator and directly to the gate, to wait again for priority boarding for our eleven-hour trip to Paris. We thanked and again tipped the person who was doing all the pushing, boarded the plane, and found our seats.

When we arrived the next morning at Charles de Gaulle Airport, we were greeted once again at the gate by another kind attendant who made me comfortable; and we set off, riding another wheelchair for the long distance from disembarking, through hallways and onto elevators, taking the airport train, stopping at passport control, and gathering our luggage before being dropped off once again to take our shuttle into Paris.

Following is what I saw that day:

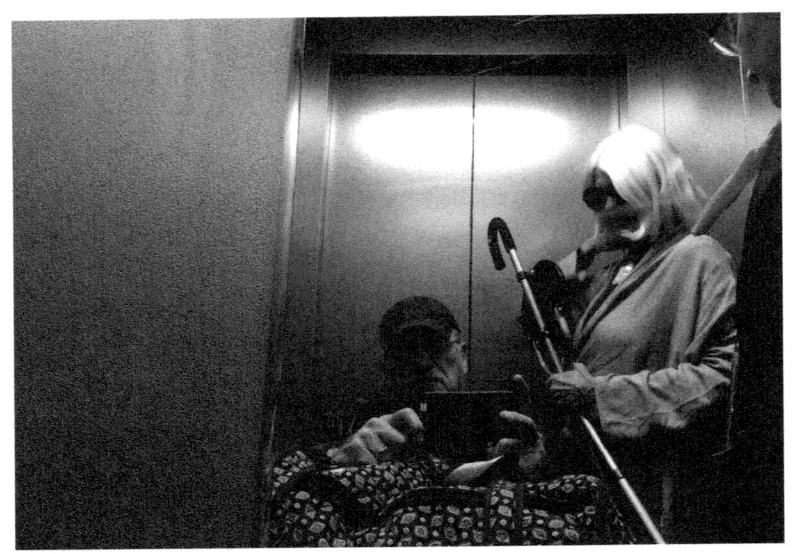

With Iris carrying my cane-seat, we set out at the Seattle airport.

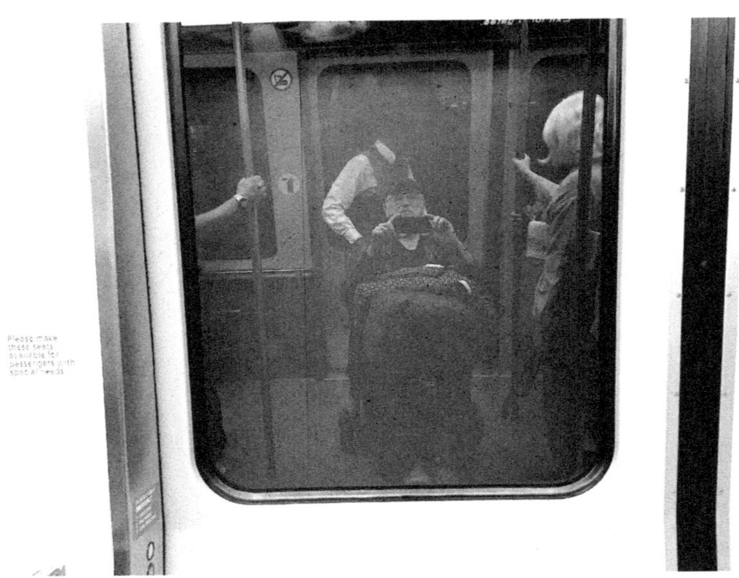

Reflection: My service assistant pushing my wheelchair onto light rail heading to the international departure terminal for our plane to Paris.

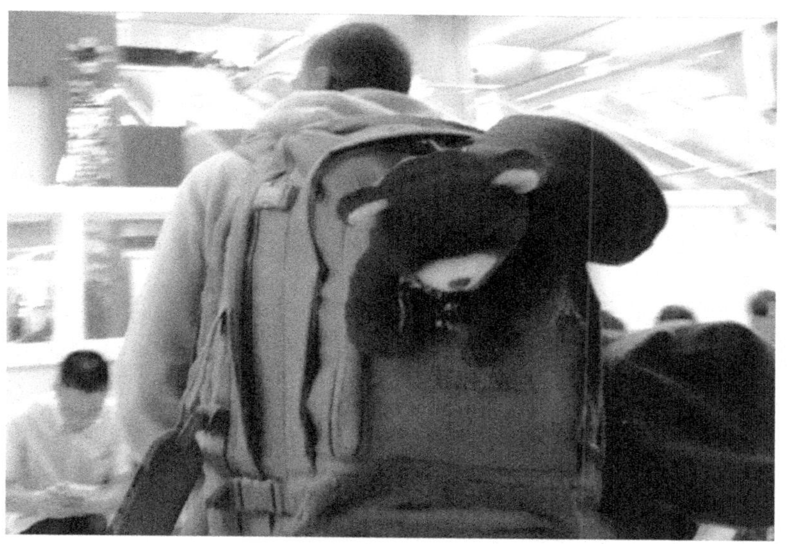

Photography from a different angle.

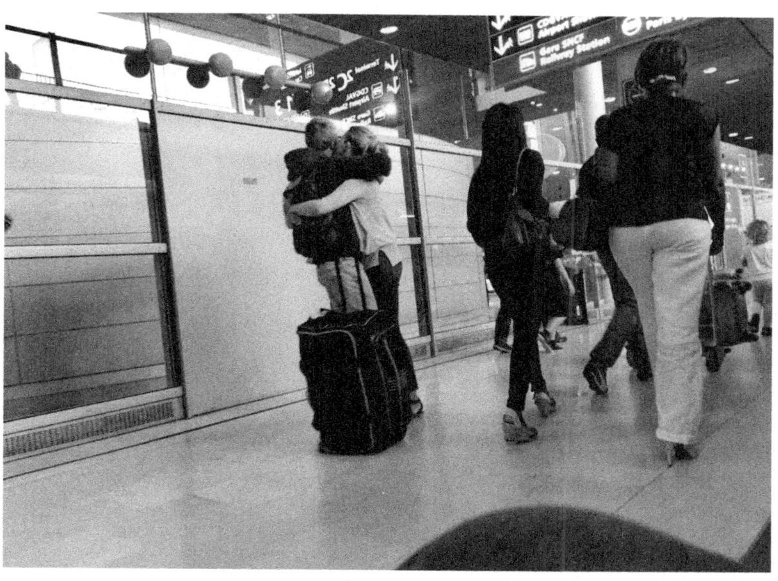

At last, Charles de Gaulle and my knee.

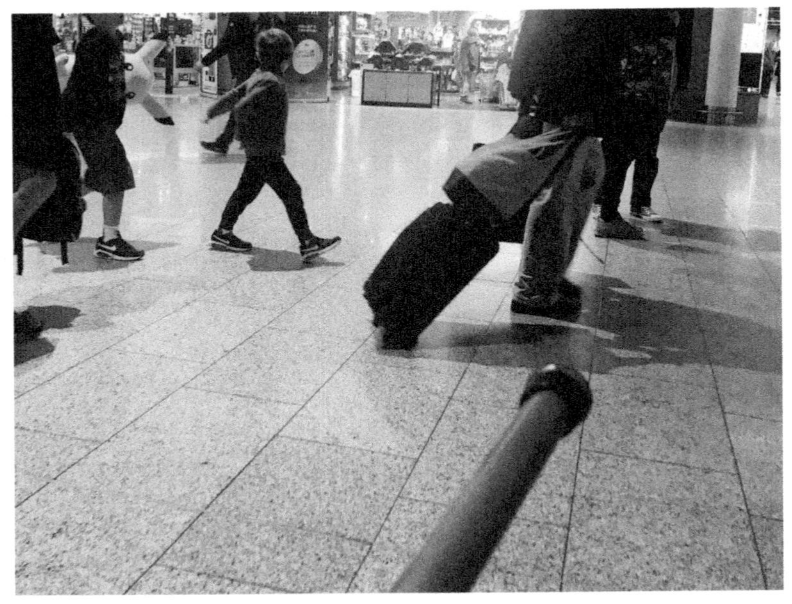

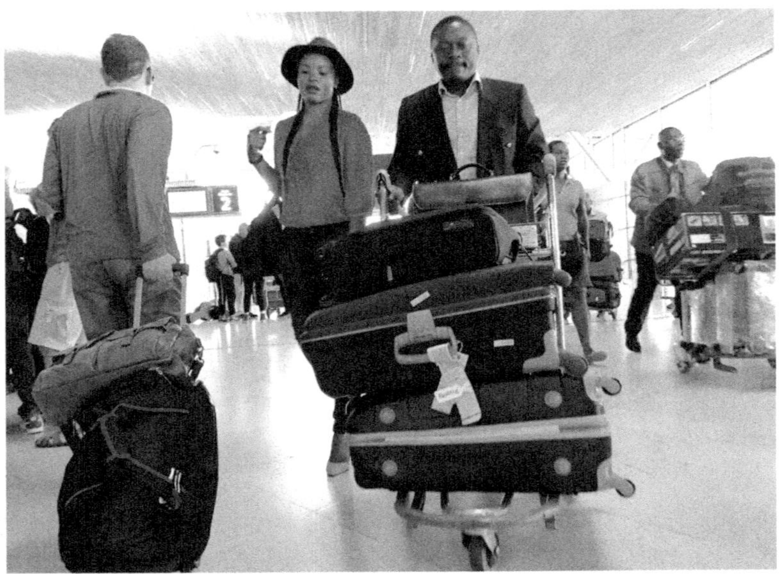

I don't think they saw me.

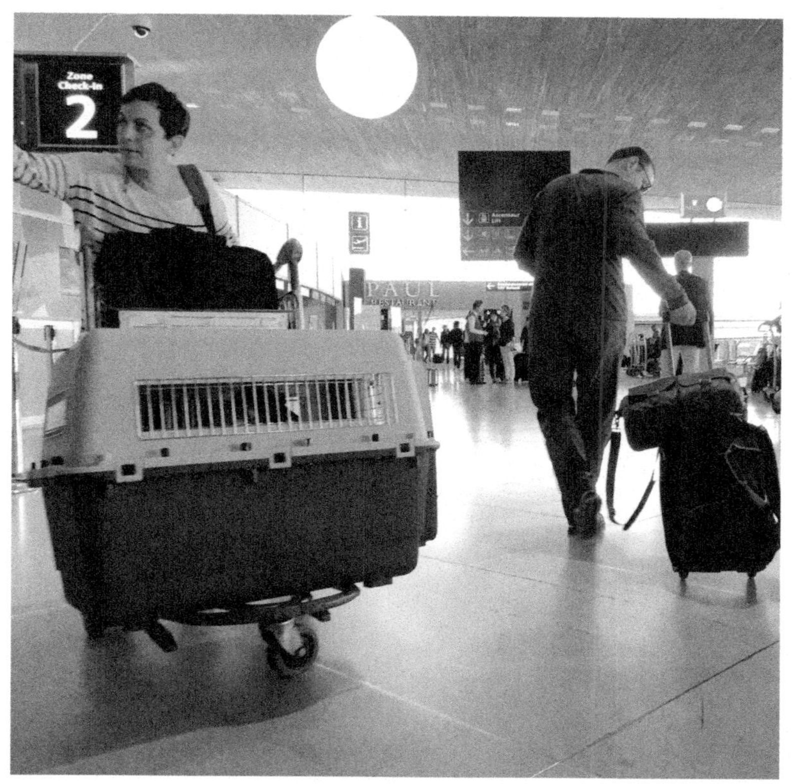

What I saw and how I felt (a little like luggage).

minimum. The story that emerges is therefore not unlike one of Noguchi's gardens, or his playground designs, or his dance sets. Space and spareness balance matter and articulation.

"An important element in both Japanese stroll gardens and Noguchi's sets was the experience of the body moving through space," Ms. Herrera writes. Arranged along the path of her chronology, Noguchi's words and deeds similarly convey their affinities without overly determining one step to the next. "If sculpture is the rock," Noguchi once wrote, "it is also the space between rocks and between the rock and a man, and the communication and contemplation between." Both artist and author leave room for us to drift around and listen.

The writer of biographies of Frida Kahlo and Arshile Gorky, two artists

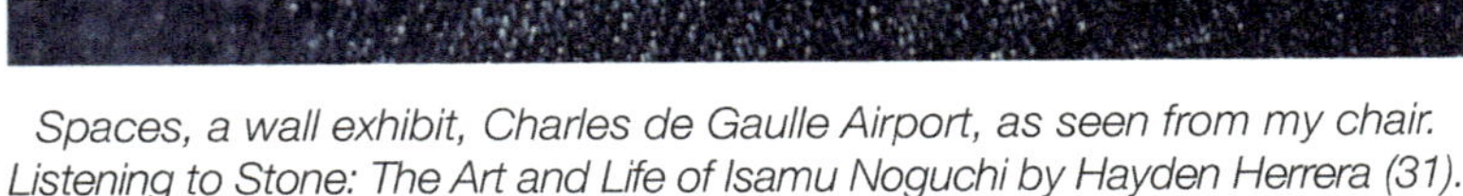

Spaces, a wall exhibit, Charles de Gaulle Airport, as seen from my chair. Listening to Stone: The Art and Life of Isamu Noguchi by Hayden Herrera (31).

CHAPTER ELEVEN

Being Camera-Ready

Noise Reduction

Being camera-ready is a familiar term, an essential preparation for a photographer. As mentioned in chapter 8, it includes the technical steps needed to determine available light, assessing characteristics of the physical location, adjusting camera settings, determining possible composition, and consciously assessing the wide range of framing possibilities needed for a successful picture-taking experience. There had been times when I thought I was ready, only to have forgotten to take off the lens cover.

"Camera-ready" in the larger sense means clearing the inside noise that I carry around with me, as well as the noise of the immediate moment that keeps me from focusing my mind. I also try to teach myself to use my photographic intuition to become more aware of what I am seeing, preparing myself to instantaneously record. Becoming focused, avoiding self-editing, I try to photograph as many digital pictures as possible, remembering I can look at them later and refine and consider before discarding. My goal is to become an objective observer as I report what I see with my camera, using the camera as a steady, reliable tool, clearing out other images and thoughts in my mind that might otherwise interfere.

Photos taken are open to later interpretation, truly enhanced by seeing more subtle things I hardly noticed at the time I took them. I look closely to see what I may have missed the first time. They become more interesting to me and are important when I have more time: a frown, shadow, or a little detail that I didn't see or hardly paid attention to at the moment that later makes it a photograph I may want to keep.

On the following page is Table 1, a summary of steps I use to become camera-ready.

Table 1: Steps I Can Take to Become Camera-Ready

— Before the shoot, <5 minutes before:

>Check the physical situation:
>Light, angle, and possible subject material.
>Check the camera and finalize settings.
>Become as clear thinking as possible.

— "Instantaneous" while shooting:

>Focus the camera.
>Take as many pictures as possible.
>No immediate self-editing.
>Snap away.
>Observe myself if possible, and self-adjust.
>Let go and clear the mind.
>Have fun.

— Afterward, ASAP (and ongoing):

>Throw out the "bad" ones.
>If any doubt about keeping, save for later.
>Ask: Why did I take this photo?
>   What was I feeling at the moment?
>   How does it make me feel now?
>Make a list of words that come to mind that
>best describe the photo.
>Make folders with the selected words:
>>Duplicate photos as needed.
>>Put in more than one file as necessary.
>>Make a memory file—random, no editing.
>>Meditate and ponder; write about possible meaning.
>
>Return to look again and stay open to possibilities.
>Trust your gut.

Learning about Myself

Sometimes when I look at my photographs, I learn far more about myself than the content alone reveals. As an example, looking at the lighthouse at the seashore (yes, I know I said in chapter 1 that I didn't like taking pictures at the seashore, but on occasion I weaken!). The photos below were blurred because I had forgotten to clean my windows when we stopped for gas. Having a bug-free windshield is easily corrected in advance the next time I am a passenger, see a shot to take, and reach for my camera. Better yet, finding a place to stop and getting outside the car has a much better chance for success than taking a photo at 55 mph. And it's safer.

The blurry windshield got me thinking that I need to also have my "personal lens" cleaned from time to time. . . not as simple. The problems of the pictures blurred by unexpected, external factors

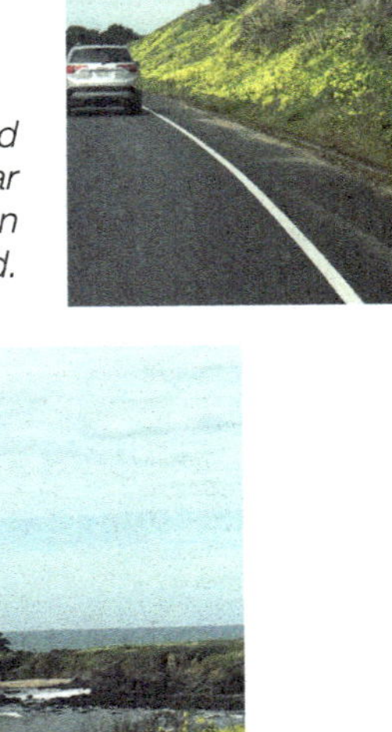

US Highway#1, unretouched photos taken from my car through the bugs on the front windshield.

are not infrequent and not easily corrected. I never thought much about the picture-taker being blurred.

I try to minimize blurring by making adjustments beforehand. Writing about it has helped me; talking with photographers about how they calm themselves; on occasion meditation, tai chi, or watching a sunset; or getting a good night's sleep. Recognizing when it happens is the first step, but making changes at the time remains a challenge.

I would add that picture-taking itself and the personal "developing" process afterward is starting to help. Gaining new insight is possible for anyone who chooses to look. I do not have perfect vision of myself nor the technical clarity that a camera can provide, but I am learning, and I do see more clearly.

Luck

My special moments are frequently accidental—a combination of luck and preparation. Here is one taken at the American Cemetery in Normandy that touched me when I looked at it later.

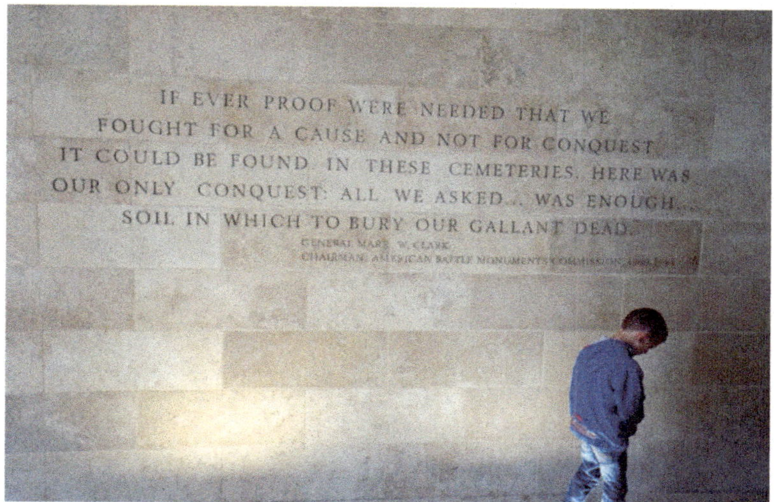

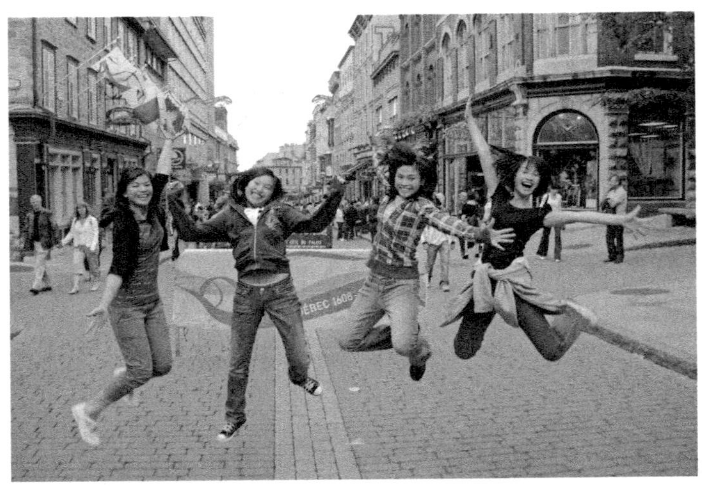

Walking along the streets of Quebec City, I came across cheerleaders jumping in front of a street poster celebrating the city's 400th anniversary.

Life Is a Snapshot

I've come to the conclusion *that life, at any one time, is really a snapshot*: taken at a single moment and combined with memories, feelings, the day's stresses, and hopes for the future. Life is full of mirrors—I am clear one moment, sometimes fogged over another. On occasion, I think one of my "mirrors" may be cracked, needing replacement, and providing only a limited vision of reality, distorted in part by life's biases and experiences.

And, here's another thought: becoming "camera-ready" is not only necessary for taking successful pictures. It might help when I am not carrying a real camera, but a metaphorical one. By using the same skills—quieting myself, being present, becoming involved and a more spontaneous participant at the time, then later reviewing these "camera-less" snapshots, can help me see the world more fully and learn to interact with the people and events of my life.

CHAPTER TWELVE

A Panoramic View

(Spring 2017)

Of course, turning the camera inward while actually taking a photo is impossible! But, when I am at home in front of the computer viewing photos, I have time to see things differently. I can reflect on what I am seeing as I use a photo to explore its possible meaning to me as a person. It happened this spring as I was writing this book.

A panoramic view taken in 2015 at the Charles de Gaulle Airport helped me connect to earlier parts of my life. On the surface, the photo was a view from one side of the bridge to the other, railroad tracks entering and leaving the airport terminal below. By "walking over the bridge" in my imagination, I could see my life from a different angle: first, where I had been; later, a period representing the present; and then, looking ahead to the far side—where I might be going (even though the real future is less certain than the photo). The surprising result was that from a "sideways" perspective I saw many new connections that weren't so apparent beforehand! Most importantly, it was all the same bridge.

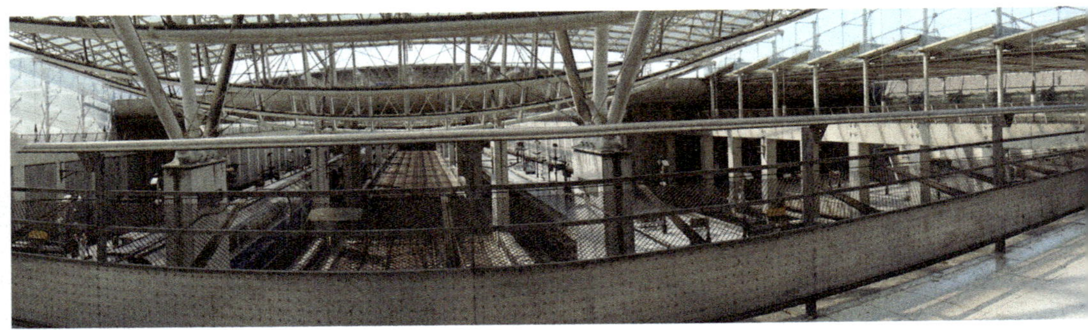

Charles de Gaulle Airport

What did I see of my life by looking sideways?

I saw an infant who spent the better part of his first two years in casts on both feet owing to a congenital anomaly called clubfoot (in medical terminology, an equino varus deformity). At the time, I was a serious candidate for surgery that might have limited my lifetime mobility; fortunately, this was a procedure I was able to avoid.

I moved forward, crossing the bridge to a point where I could see myself accepted in 1956 to the University of Colorado School of Medicine, choosing pediatrics after my first year and spending as much time as I could doing pediatric research and taking additional electives in clinical care of infants and children while in medical school. Postgraduate work included a residency in Pediatrics and a fellowship in Adolescent Medicine, though I was unable to serve afterward in the armed services because of my own disability.

I observed certain professional landmarks later in my life: becoming a faculty member at USC in 1963; helping to start a new field of adolescent medicine; learning and writing about humanistic practices in medicine and health; becoming a public health administrator for a children's chronic disease program; returning to teach in medical school; serving as a full-time associate dean at USC involved with curriculum development and faculty advancement; and, finally, before retiring in 2000, completing my career as Department Chair of Pediatrics, returning to the same hospital where I started my academic career.

Interestingly, my lifetime interests to that point did not include photography.

Looking more fully from the vantage point of the "bridge," I remembered a powerful emotional episode in my thirties, when I had a series of ten Rolfing sessions, a form of deep-tissue massage. (32) Some quite painful, they were meant to explore possible connections between my body and "memories" stored inside. One of the sessions involved my lower extremities, causing a powerful painful physical as well as emotional response to what might have been the earliest memories of my clubfeet, not unlike a kind of posttraumatic stress syndrome. (33) As I felt the physical pain of the deep massage, I became very sad and started to cry, crying that continued, increasing in strength, experiencing memories previously unavailable to me that had been locked inside all those years. I asked the therapist to stop.

I am not so sure that I can explain all that happened, but it felt like I had returned to that early time in my life, releasing memories stored inside when both feet were in casts. It must have been quite an emotional experience for that little boy, as I remembered it later during the Rolfing session; and again last spring, when the memory surfaced as part of revisiting this experience from the perspective of the panorama photo.

I continued my sideways look. It didn't seem so unrelated when I returned to Los Angeles in 1978 as medical director of a county, state, and federal program that provided inpatient and outpatient medical, social, and physical therapy services for children with special needs including handicapping conditions like clubfoot.

I realized, despite all that had transpired, I never thought
of myself as being disabled. But that was changing with
spinal stenosis when I looked at my recent experiences as a
photographer: two years ago traveling by wheelchair and my
class in Paris the same year.

First, despite what I thought was a healthy life, my body had
finally caught up with me, and I was now facing an unknown
future of physical limitation. My wheelchair trips through airports
helped me understand what might be in store for me—still able
to take pictures, but not able to move around as much as I
had before. Assisted travel helped me experience a world with
limitations and wonder realistically about my future mobility.

Second, the course in Paris helped me understand I have to be
an active observer of life, rather than distant and passive, "safe"
behind my telephoto lens. I saw again that photos taken from
a distance did not require me to interact directly with people.
I had chosen to take photos of life, but was not necessarily
living it. It was not a conscious act to withdraw and only observe.
It just happened. I now saw how very easy it might be for me
to finish my own personal life journey assuming the label of an
aging, disabled person from a distance. I hadn't fully realized that
that was how I was already living in some ways, even before the
wide-angle photos that I learned to take that summer.

Third, the irony of finding Jon being wheeled around Paris
by his father wasn't lost. I knew I had to figure out a way to
continue taking pictures of Jon at the time. Offering my camera
on impulse changed our relationship—I had found a way to
relate to him by sitting on the ground and having him take
my picture. Not only did the quality of our interaction become
positive, I was able to record it.

Coming back to the bridge and reviewing my lifetime as a
whole, I connected it all: my earliest moments of life when
mobility was an issue, becoming a pediatrician caring for

adolescents, undergoing Rolfing later in my life and re-
experiencing early childhood memories, leading a public health
program for handicapped children, becoming a photographer
after I retired, developing my own mobility issues in my eighties,
deciding to be a more active participant by taking close-
up pictures instead of being a distant photographer using
a telephoto lens, finding a young person with a disability to
photograph and finding a way to engage him successfully by
asking him to take my picture—these no longer seemed like
random events in isolation from one another.

My life now makes more internal sense, viewed from this angle.
There is a remarkable consistency when my experiences
are linked like cars on a train crossing the bridge. I leave the
speculation and further interpretations of these life events for
me to think about in the future and for others to ponder more.
Regardless of what other possible interpretations may surface
in the future, my personal work as a photographer helped me to
explain and connect with what has happened during my lifetime.

As a result, I am committed to altering my course across the
bridge. Trusting myself, taking risks to reach out to engage with
people and looking for new ways to photograph that might
make them more comfortable (me, too), and later, by using
photos and my imagination, to continue an inward look at
what they might mean to me—a powerful tool to help my own
process of self-discovery.

A search for a photography of the self can be defined as: *the
interactions between a photographer and his inner and outer
worlds, permitting a fuller understanding of the learning that
occurs when the camera is turned inward, by providing insight
and awareness and creating a clearer vision, thus enhancing
the skills and beauty of a photographer's life and art.*

CHAPTER THIRTEEN

Final Thoughts

My own review process is continuous. As I look more closely, I see that continuity plus something else, a direction of my intent throughout. I can see how much I have always been committed to finding the connections people make to their daily lives; connecting with them means entering those lives myself as I seek ways to photograph and make contact with the people who are my subjects. I have learned to dial down my own priorities and goals and to submit to the task of realizing my subjects through film. Redefining my identity so that I am not always prioritizing myself is for me what it means to be a successful photographer. The degree of my success at this, paradoxically, is measured by how much I have learned about myself in that process.

I can see now that obtaining new and different views of my own concerns has become a large part of what I get back from giving so much focused attention, holding a camera, when I look into the lives of others. Most of all, though, I have learned to savor and to treasure. I have learned that becoming a successful photographer begins by discovering the joy in taking pictures, without any expectations, recognition, or material outcome. Photography for me is a verb, like love; it acts to reaffirm my commitment to living a purposeful life.

My primary teachers in this endeavor have been the photographers of the past. But the photographers of today have taught me firsthand about camera techniques and new ways of engagement. And most importantly, my subjects have inspired me in the art of looking at their lives. From the people I've seen that I have photographed, spoken to, and observed, I learned what it means to look at another person, and I have learned to see myself that way as well. I have realized how much more depth I have, both as a photographer and as a person, than I ever imagined before I took up photography.

I have learned there is a special chemistry between the one taking the pictures and the people at the other end of the camera that can, under certain circumstances, catalyze a human connection. A search for that path to connectedness has become a part of my life. I don't try too hard to connect with the people. Rather, I try to find the chemistry that already exists between us, and let that make our connection happen. On occasion, when that chemistry is found, the connection that results can be captured on camera and reflected in my photographs. Then the viewers can see for themselves what I found special enough about another life to demonstrate via a photograph. They can then identify the universal human qualities that I found to illuminate with my camera.

Writing this book has been helpful in getting me to see the continuity within my own oeuvre. Setting down these reflections has reminded me that photos are memories that don't fade. I am learning to let them become my continuous reference library for personal reflection. Memories and emotions have of course surfaced when I have looked back at past photos I've taken. Such moments of recall teach me that I really can trust my photographic intuition to hone in on what is salient. I can snap away and not worry about getting a perfect picture because I know that an instinct for what's interesting has been guiding my hand. I have also learned that I am a feeling person, much more sensitive than I had thought, more vulnerable, and yet I find it is also possible for me to become a sturdy participant observer. Photography enables me to get involved with others and see how that involvement affects me as a human being.

For the future, I want to become part of a continuing story that might be more than a single shoot. I plan to keep looking for events connected to a cause or to telling stories in more detail. I hope to discover an issue, a topic, or a simple story that needs telling in more depth that is ongoing and allows me to be part of the long-term story. I am optimistic it will come, though I am in a race of sorts given the realities of an older age.

And, the questions continue: How to find pictures that touch others? Photograph special moments? Discover life around me and become more involved? Use photography as a way to learn more about myself? Find the wisdom I continue to search for?

I am not as afraid to reach out and introduce myself. I acknowledge that sometimes I will hear a "no" and have to decide whether to continue and, if so, how to continue to relate. Like my experience with Jon and his father: our special moment helped me take a panoramic look at my own life.

This book is meant to be a guide, a way to discover that taking pictures can offer much more than creating the art of the camera; it also provides a way to look inward, stopping when you feel it makes sense to do so. By looking again at your own material and carefully examining the photos you have taken, you may discover new ways to photograph and choose to take the pictures of the future and, in the process, find the ones that have special meaning for you. My hope is that you will take good notes as you go along, share your thoughts and feelings with others, and keep on shooting pictures.

What have I learned from the last twelve years? My objective viewer might say the following to me, as shown in Table 2.

Table 2: What My Objective Viewer Might Say to Me

- It's not technology that matters. Forget about f-stops and light meters; all that stuff is done automatically these days. It's your heart.

- You've found a place to take pictures. Take a trip to Paris with your camera; then take another one. Find other places and settings that speak to you.

- Keep looking at photographs of the classic artists of the last century. Black and white speaks to you; it is your medium.

- Trust your gut feelings: Learn to go with what the photo wants to say—don't self-edit.

- You are the photographer; you are the only one to make the decisions about your work. Listen to others, but no one else can make them for you.

- Laugh a lot at yourself and your situation—one of the best ways to learn.

- Don't be a spectator, be a participant observer.

- Think, act, and become an objective photographer.

- Try to talk with your subjects so they can participate in the picture-taking process.

- Don't forget that this is a work of art you're making: you have to be able to frame the picture and focus the camera so that everything in the shot is put in proper perspective.

- Not everybody is going to like your work. It just takes one fan—yourself—to give you the heart to continue.

- You don't have to carry a camera to see and take "virtual pictures" that may become meaningful images to you. Your eye is even more sophisticated than a Leica camera.

- If the picture you took speaks to you, it will speak to others too.

- Few photographers ever made a fortune taking good pictures; we are all fortunate to have them though.

- No one single picture can tell whole the story of your photographic experiences. Ask yourself, what does your body of work say to those who look at your pictures?

- Hundreds of photography books come out each year. You want to know why anyone might need to see yours.

- Be kind to yourself.

In the larger sense, photography becomes a gateway to self-realization, i.e., "fulfillment by oneself of the possibilities of one's character or personality." (34)

I continue to search for a photography of the self and a way toward my own self-realization.

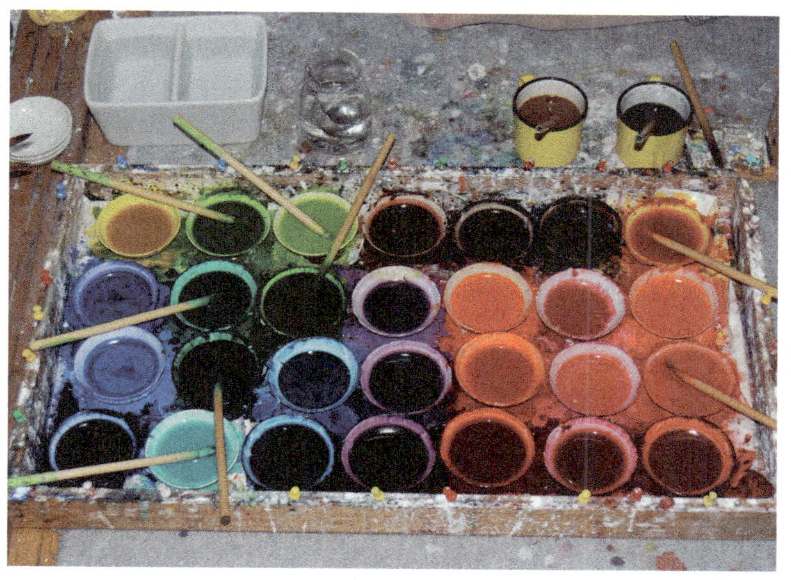

The limitless "palate" of photography.
Japan

References

1. Joseph Nicéphore Niépce, *View from the Window at Le Gras*, 1826, Wikipedia.
2. Louis Daguerre, 1839, Wikipedia.
3. *Wild Beauty: Photography of the Columbia River Gorge, 1867–1957.* (Northwest Photography, OSU, 2008).
4. Van Deren Coke, *The Painter and the Photograph* (University of New Mexico Press, 1964).
5. David Hockney and Martin Gayford, *A History of Pictures: From the Cave to the Computer Screen* (London: Thames and Hudson Ltd., and New York: Abrams, 2016).
6. Peter Stepan, *50 Photographers You Should Know* (Munich, London, New York: Prestel, 2011).
7. Ian Jeffrey, *How to Read a Photograph: Lessons Learned from Master Photographers* (New York: Abrams, 2008).
8. *Phantom*, a recent landscape photo by Peter Lik, sold for $6.5 million in 2014 (*Artnet News*, 2014).
9. The field of photojournalism, in its narrowest sense, uses images to tell a news story, and has been described as "the art or practice of communicating news by photographs, especially in magazines. It has come to include documentary photography, social documentary photography, street photography, and celebrity photography," Wikipedia.
10. Clive Scott, *Street Photography from Atget to Cartier-Bresson* (London: I. B. Tauris Ltd, 2007).
11. Edward Steichen, *The Family of Man*, An Exhibit, NY MOMA, January 24–May 8, 1955 (New York: R. R. Donnelley & Sons).
12. Henri Cartier-Bresson, *The Decisive Moment* (New York: Simon Schuster, 1952), Introduction, xiv,
13. *Eliot Porter, Intimate Landscapes*, Metropolitan Museum of Art, Dutton, NY, 1979.
14. *The Work of Atget, The Art of Old Paris*, Vol. II of IV, p. 9–32, MOMA, NY, NY, 1982.
15. *Ansel Adams, An Autobiography* (Boston: Little, Brown and Company, 1985).

16. John Maloof, *Vivian Maier, Street Photographer* (Brooklyn, NY: Powerhouse Books, 2011).
17. *Walker Evans,* MOMA, NY, in association with Princeton University Press, Princeton, New York, 2000.
18. Edouard Boubat, *It's a Wonderful Life* (Paris: Assouline, 1996).
19. From an interview of Cartier-Bresson by Dorothy Newman (as quoted in his obituary of August 3, 2004, the *New York Times,* Michael Kimmelman).
20. Josef Koudelka, *Gypsies* (New York: Aperture Foundation, Artbook/D.A.P., 1970, revised 2011).
21. Definitions: JPEG (Joint Photographic Experts Group) and RAW, Wikipedia.
22. *Digital Photopro* magazine, May 4, 2015.
23. Dale Garell, *People I've Seen*, April 2010, Blurb.
24. Garell, *People I've Seen II*, February 2011, Blurb.
25. Garell, *People I've Seen II* (Revised), October 2012, Blurb.
26. Garell, *To Dream . . . Travels to South America*, July 2011, Blurb.
27. Garell, *Children I've Seen*, Fall 2012, Blurb.
28. Chinadaily.com. 04/04/2015, Cultural differences between China and the US.
29. A Code of Ethics of the National Press Photographers Association (NPPA) prepared in 1991 addresses the issues of digital changes in photographs and sets standards of behavior in visual storytelling for members (NPPA.org).
30. Peter Turnley, *Parisians* (New York: Abbeville Press, 2000).
31. Hayden Herrera, *Listening to Stone: The Art and Life of Isamu Noguchi* (New York: Ferra, Straus, and Giroux, 2015), Charles de Gaulle Airport.
32. Rolfing is a form of alternative medicine originally developed by Ida Rolf (1896–1979), sometimes called Structural Integration, Wikipedia.
33. Bessel van der Kolk, *The Body Keeps the Score: Brain, Mind and Body in the Healing of Trauma* (Viking Press, 2014).
34. *Merriam-Webster Collegiate Dictionary*, 2015.

Acknowledgments

Like Boubat (18) I remain young through taking photos, finding special moments that touch me and discovering how important photography and the process of taking photos has become to me. I couldn't have written this book any earlier in my life. Photography has led to such productive and happy activities, a few frustrations at times, added energy to my life as well as the almost continuous challenges of learning more about myself. I know I am not fully aware of all the possible connections and wiring that have occurred during this process. I still have much work to do.

There are many people I would like to acknowledge with my thanks. First, to my wife, Iris, for her patience, coaching, and being my muse and good listener whenever I needed it. I do very much appreciate her thoughtful comments on my story and the pictures that illustrate it, as well as the careful editing she has provided for my manuscript.

And, to my family, immediate and more distant, to those continuously expanding circles of people we call our family, to the many others who have shared their life stories and listened to mine.

My thanks to William Hoard and his team at BookCreate for his patience, wisdom, and ability to translate words and pictures into a coherent whole. And, to Barbara Fandrich for her careful editing and continuous encouragement to tell my story.

To many others who have provided guidance and advice:

Shirley Polovy, Art Coach, who asked the first hard questions;

Richard Gadd, Director and Curator, Weston Gallery, Carmel, California, who quietly suggested a pathway;

Troy Peters, Master Printer, Urban Digital Color, San Francisco,

California, who taught me, refined my work and helped me understand whose pictures they truly are;

Professeure Aime Benichou, Curator, Peintres du Medicines, at the Sorbonne who took a chance;

Ghislaine Augier of Bordeaux, France, our longtime friend, attorney, and my first "agent";

Peter Turnley, photojournalist, whose course taught me about the art of photography, but even more about myself;

Jacqueline Bugnion, Lausanne, Switzerland, who has graciously read this manuscript, and who along with her husband, Jean-Robert, found a home for my art and has followed my work for the last ten years;

Marjorie Shaevitz, La Jolla, California, admissionpossible.com, Huffington Post blog, for her listening and helpful guidance, friendship, and expert editing, and for sharing her own writing experiences;

Rachel Gribby, who works at OHSU in Portland, and is a PT's physical therapist whose encouragement and support continues to make a difference in my own clinical course.

To those early photographers who inspired their audiences with their black and white photos, for their photographic creativity and the genius they share with those who have followed them, now well into the twenty-first century. I am in awe of their work!

To the people I've seen whose pictures I have taken. And, to the many others who have seen my art, with my hope that it has touched them and made a difference in their lives.

To the photographers who have shared their work with me, their hopes and dreams as well as their frustrations.

And, finally, to all who love photography.

CPSIA information can be obtained
at www.ICGtesting.com
Printed in the USA
BVOW05s0147030118
504274BV00005B/7/P